THE RHEINGOLD ROUTE

Arthur Maling

D1426844

LONDON
VICTOR GOLLANCZ LTD
1979

ISBN 0 575 02713 4

479027707

00195488

m0320288LC

Printed in Great Britain by
Lowe & Brydone Printers Limited, Thetford, Norfolk

For
the McClures—
Jim, Lorly, James, Jr., Alistair, and Kirsten—
with all best

THE RHEINGOLD ROUTE

1

"Mr. Cochran?"

"Speaking."

"Mr. *John* Cochran?"

"Yes."

"My name is Evans. Er—Peter Evans. I have some business I'd like to—er—discuss with you."

Cochran frowned. The name wasn't familiar to him. Neither was the voice. "Who gave you my number, Mr. Evans?"

"A Mr. Arlen. A Mr.—er—David Arlen."

Cochran's frown deepened. Arlen had never in the past given his telephone number to anyone. Furthermore, Arlen was in Spain at the moment. "What kind of business do you have in mind?"

"It's nothing I'd care to—er—go into over the telephone. May I come to your flat?"

"No."

Evans sounded shocked. "Really, Mr. Cochran, I—I don't

know what to say. I'm quite respectable, you know. I mean, I'm sure that Mr. Arlen would want you to meet with me."

"Then I suggest you have him call me and tell me so himself."

"But I can't. I mean, Mr. Arlen is in Spain. I—I can assure you I'm quite—er—reputable."

Cochran leaned against the edge of the table. Apparently the man did know Arlen. "No doubt you are," he said, trying to imagine how a man who spoke like Evans would look. The picture that came to mind included a starched white collar, spectacles with thick lenses, and a perpetually furrowed brow.

"Oh, it's so awkward to explain over the telephone! I mean, if we could meet . . . Really, Mr. Cochran, don't you think you might be—er—making a mistake?"

"So might you, Mr. Evans. I haven't even said that I know a David Arlen. But if I do, and if he wants us to get together, he can arrange it when he gets back."

"But that's not likely to be for some time. I mean, two or three weeks. And the matter I have to discuss with you is, well, urgent. I realize that you've just returned from one of your—er—trips and that—"

Cochran tightened his grip on the telephone. The information that he'd just returned from a trip could have come from only one source: Arlen. "What did you say?"

"That you might be, well, tired. Still I thought—I hoped—"

"O.K., we'll meet."

"We will? Oh, splendid! I'll come to your flat, then?"

"No, we'll make it somewhere else. Some public place."

"Of course. A public place. Excellent."

The more public, the better, Cochran thought. "How about the buffet at Victoria Air Terminal?"

"The buffet at Victoria Air Terminal. Most suitable. At what time?"

"How about four o'clock this afternoon?"

"Quite convenient. Really. Four o'clock."

"How will I recognize you?"

"Recognize me? Oh dear, I see what you mean. Well, I— I'm rather tall and I—er—"

"Never mind. *You* look for *me*. I'll be wearing a tan turtle-neck and a brown leather jacket and I'll be drinking a cup of coffee. I'll have a magazine with me. A foreign magazine. *Réalités.*"

"*Réalités.* Brown leather jacket. Coffee. I'll remember. Really, Mr. Cochran, I—"

Cochran hung up. He wished that there were some way of getting in touch with Arlen. Two or three weeks, Evans had said. Was that the truth? Arlen hadn't told *him* how long he'd be away; all he'd said, when they'd parted in Geneva, was that he was on his way to Spain and would call him when he got back to London. But that was usual. To Arlen, John Cochran was just one of the checkers on the checker-board, an object to be moved about during the game and kept in a box the rest of the time.

He put Arlen out of his mind and tried to make something of the conversation itself. Respectable. Reputable. Shocked at not being allowed to come to the flat. Unaccustomed to describing himself. And, despite the faltering manner, not easily put off.

The fragments formed a pattern. That of a man who was sure of his acceptability and who, although he seemed weak-willed, was used to getting what he wanted.

Watch out for the shy ones, Cochran reminded himself; they're often the most determined.

He started to consult the telephone directory, then decided not to. There were undoubtedly a lot of P. Evanses, and the addresses would tell him nothing. Besides, he didn't know that the man was a Londoner. Or, for that matter, that Evans was his real name.

He sighed and went to the window. It was still raining.

Except for a parking inspector who was putting a warning notice on the windshield of a Ford Cortina, Basil Street was deserted. Sundays are lonely days, he thought. December is a lonely month. He stopped short of adding that he was a lonely man, however; he'd concluded long ago that he deserved no pity, least of all his own.

Yet he couldn't help thinking that it would be nice if there were someone he could occasionally talk things over with. Someone he could trust.

There wasn't, though.

And it was with this fact firmly in mind that he put on his leather jacket, picked up the copy of *Réalités* from the table and went out to find a taxi to take him to the Victoria Air Terminal.

2

There were times, he'd learned, when it was best not to be curious about the future, not to anticipate. So he forced himself to concentrate on the immediate moment, making a small ceremony of unwrapping the cube of sugar, dropping it into the coffee and stirring it until it dissolved. Then he opened the damp magazine and turned the pages until he came to the article about the château in Auvergne. He'd bought the magazine at the Gare de Lyon on his last trip through Paris, and with the aid of a French-English dictionary he'd already translated the first two paragraphs of that particular article; now he began to go over them without the dictionary, pronouncing each word to himself as he imagined it should be pronounced and trying to remember what it meant. It was an exercise not in French but in self-control.

And as such it was hard. His thoughts kept breaking loose, and he kept having to pull them back.

After a few minutes his eyes wandered. The buffet was

crowded, mostly with foreigners. At the table to his right was a party of blacks who were conversing happily in the soft accents of the Caribbean. At the table to his left, a family of Pakistanis—father, mother and two children—swathed in flight bags from half a dozen airlines. And at the table beyond them, two dark-skinned young men with Vandyke beards and Levantine features.

He'd picked the right place, he thought. Everyone was pre-occupied with his own departure time and his own belongings.

He sipped some coffee and dragged his attention back to the printed page. "Completed in the year 1748, the park with its circular arrangement of . . ." What were *arbrisseaux?* He couldn't recall. And again his eyes strayed. This time in the direction of the stairway by which he'd come up from the lobby.

A man was standing on the top step, shaking the water from his umbrella and looking around. A man of slightly more than average height.

Cochran raised the magazine a few inches and pretended to read.

"Er—Mr. Cochran?" he heard presently.

Slowly he put the magazine down beside the coffee cup. Then, just as slowly, he nodded.

"I'm Evans. Er—Peter Evans. May I—er—sit down?"

Cochran extended an open palm toward the other chair, and Evans, as uncertain in his movements as he was in his speech, deposited himself onto it in stages. He wasn't wearing a starched white collar or spectacles with thick lenses and he didn't have a furrowed brow. He was a clean-shaven man of about forty-five with a deep cleft in his chin and blue eyes that brimmed with earnestness.

He gave Cochran a nervous little smile and said, "I don't want you to have the wrong impression. I mean, I'm afraid I—er—misrepresented myself over the telephone. I mean—that is, I—well, what I'm trying to say is that I don't actually

6

know David Arlen. That is, I haven't actually *met* him. Actually, you see, it's my solicitor who knows him. My solicitor is the one who—er—suggested I call you. I—I hope you don't mind. I mean—"

"Who's your solicitor?"

"Michael Garwood. I don't think that the name—er—means anything to you. Does it?"

Cochran shook his head.

"I mean, I hope—"

"Why didn't he call me himself?"

"Well, you see, the problem is really mine. I mean, I'm the one who—who has to—" He paused to wipe away the perspiration that was forming along his upper lip. "To accept the—er—responsibility."

Cochran said nothing.

"I hope you understand," Evans went on, his expression still earnest. "I mean, Uncle Michael does intend to meet you. He—he's *expecting* you. Tomorrow afternoon at two o'clock."

Cochran decided that his original estimate was right. A man who assumed he was going to get his way. "Is that a fact?"

"Yes. Two o'clock."

Cochran drank some coffee, which was now cold. Then, pushing the cup aside, he said, "Would you mind telling me what the hell this is all about?"

Evans drew back and gave him a hurt look. But the look didn't last. "Well, actually," he explained, "I'm trying to. It—it's just that I—er—I'm not very good at this sort of thing, I'm afraid. I mean, I've never dealt with anyone like you before."

Cochran raised an eyebrow.

"No offense, I hope," Evans added quickly.

"Why don't you just say what's on your mind?"

Evans took a deep breath. "Well, yes, I suppose that would

be best. I have some money I want moved. Quite a lot of money. Three hundred and fifty thousand pounds."

Cochran smiled. "Good luck," he said. "I won't stand in your way."

"But—but you don't understand, Mr. Cochran. I want you to move it for me."

"You called a wrong number, buddy."

"I know—I mean, Uncle Michael knows—that you're Arlen's courier. Uncle Michael is Arlen's solicitor."

Cochran considered various responses. None of them seemed adequate.

"Uncle Michael is very reputable," Evans offered as the clincher.

Arlen had never mentioned having a lawyer. Yet undoubtedly he did have one. "I don't know a David Arlen," Cochran said flatly. "But if I did, and if I were what you said I am, you can be goddamn sure that he wouldn't loan me out. Not to you, not to your Uncle Michael, not to anybody."

"The fee will be three thousand pounds," Evans said. "That's—er—twice what Arlen pays you."

Exactly twice. "I don't know how to put it plainer, Evans. You're barking up the wrong tree."

"Plus expenses, of course."

The Pakistani family had got up from the table and was rearranging the flight bags before leaving. Cochran decided that it was time for him to leave too. He reached for the magazine. "It's been nice meeting you," he said.

"Oh dear!" Evans exclaimed when he saw Cochran push his chair back. "Let me give you Uncle Michael's card. Otherwise you won't know where to go. I mean—"

"No need." Cochran tucked his magazine under his arm and stood up.

"But really, Mr. Cochran, I hate to sound—er—insistent, but it would be, well, dangerous for you to refuse."

Cochran looked down at the seated man. "I love people who threaten me."

"It would, though," Evans said, not flinching from the gaze. "I mean, the next time you attempted to leave England you'd be arrested."

"I beg your pardon?"

"Really, you would. That's the truth. I mean, the Customs and Excise people would—er—be interested in knowing about the money you—er—well, you know what I mean. And Uncle Michael, being in a position to, well, tell them, if you know what I mean."

Cochran forced himself to smile. "You don't look like a blackmailer," he said. "Not in the least."

Perspiration was again forming on Evans's upper lip. "But I'm not. I mean, I don't want to be. It's simply that I—I have this money that I really do want taken to Switzerland, and Uncle Michael suggested you." He wiped his lip, then reached into the pocket of his raincoat. "I'll give you his card."

Cochran accepted the card. The address was in New Square, Lincoln's Inn.

Evans heaved a sigh of relief. "I do wish it had been easier," he said. "But you will be there at two o'clock—er—won't you?"

"I haven't the faintest idea," Cochran said.

But as he made his way between the tables and started down the steps to the lobby he felt a growing certainty that he would be there. That he had no choice in the matter.

3

O'Rourke dropped the stub of his cigarette onto the pavement, ground it out with the heel of his boot and walked into the sandwich bar.

He hadn't liked the look of the place from the outside, and he didn't like it from the inside either. It was inferior.

The man behind the counter was slicing a tomato. O'Rourke watched him. The slices were so thin that they were almost transparent. It took a sharp knife to make slices that thin—a sharp knife and a sharp eye for profit. The man had to be a sodding foreigner.

"Coffee—white," he said when the man finally noticed him.

At the back of the shop was a steep, narrow stairway. O'Rourke mounted the steps with his cup of coffee and found himself in a small dining room with benches along two walls and windows overlooking Chancery Lane and Bream's Buildings. The tables and stools were bolted to the floor, as if to prevent their being stolen. The floor itself was uneven, and the linoleum with which it was covered had bald spots.

Demeaning, he thought.

He chose a table at the far end and seated himself with his back to one of the windows, so that he could keep an eye on the entire area. It was the sort of room that made him uncomfortable. Aside from its air of shabbiness, it was hazardous; the stairway was at the wrong end and wasn't wide enough. Nevertheless he assumed a posture of unconcern, with his legs crossed and one arm resting carelessly on the table in such a way as to show his bracelet. The bracelet was new, and he was pleased with it. For years he'd wanted a bracelet of fourteen-karat gold.

The soiled plates and cups on the tables around him indicated that there had been customers in the room earlier. Secretaries probably, or clerks. Maybe a few lawyers too, en route from their offices to the courts. And no doubt there would be even more customers during the lunch hour. However, the man he was to meet had chosen wisely—the brief period between late morning coffee and early lunch.

He wondered whether the man's name really was Garwood and whether it would make any difference what his name was.

His thoughts were interrupted by footsteps on the stairs. But it was only the sandwich-maker come to collect the dirty dishes and place them on the dumbwaiter. O'Rourke noted with distaste that the man smoothed out the paper napkins that weren't sufficiently stained and put them back in the glass container.

Bloody wop, he thought.

The sandwich-maker returned to the ground floor, and O'Rourke lit a cigarette. Then, resuming the posture of unconcern, he simply waited.

The wait was short. Heavier footsteps on the stairs announced the arrival of someone other than the sandwich-maker, and a moment later a stranger appeared. The stranger fitted the description O'Rourke had been given, and evidently he knew what O'Rourke would look like, for he came right up to him and said, "Kenneth O'Rourke, I believe."

O'Rourke smiled lazily and nodded.

The stranger didn't introduce himself. He merely put his cup of tea on the table and sat down on one of the stools. "What have you been told?" he asked.

O'Rourke blew a stream of smoke over the man's shoulder and said, "That you have a job you'd like me to do."

"Anything else?"

"That your name is Garwood and you're a solicitor."

The stranger studied him.

He met the gaze with one that was equally appraising. Sixty-five if a day, he thought. Eyes like a bloody hawk. Arrogant bastard, probably. "Do you like what you see?" he asked finally.

The stranger picked up his teacup, but before he tasted the tea he nodded.

O'Rourke wasn't sure whether the nod meant approval of himself or confirmation of his facts. He put out his cigarette and, noticing that some ash had fallen onto his suede overcoat, he brushed it off. *"Are* you Garwood?"

Garwood put his cup down, hesitated, then said, "You have been correctly informed."

Likes fancy language, O'Rourke added to his assessment. He decided not to ask for proof of identity. The man did exactly match the description Trumper had given him, and Trumper was reliable. According to Trumper, it was Garwood and the barrister Garwood had retained who had got him acquitted. And in Trumper's case the acquittal had been nothing short of a miracle.

Evidently Garwood was feeling some uncertainty too, for he said, "Alfred Trumper assures me you can be trusted."

"Likewise with you," O'Rourke replied.

"Then we understand each other."

O'Rourke smiled and lit another cigarette. "What's the job?"

"Recovering some money that's been stolen."

O'Rourke frowned. Recovering stolen property was something he'd never done before. "Recovering it from where?"

"From an American who calls himself John Cochran."

"Where's he got it?"

"I don't know at the moment. But I do know that he intends to smuggle it over to Switzerland."

"Um. And you want me to get it back before he skips the country."

"No, I want you to get it back *after* he skips the country."

O'Rourke took the cigarette from between his lips and regarded it thoughtfully. He wondered what would happen if he jammed the glowing tip against Garwood's hand. It would raise a lovely blister. It would also show the old bastard that Kenneth O'Rourke was no one to be devious with. But he dismissed the idea as imprudent. "I don't understand," he said.

"I emphasize 'after,'" Garwood said. "In other words, I want you to recover the money on the Continent."

"You mean go abroad?" O'Rourke asked incredulously.

"Why should that surprise you? Trumper assures me that you have a passport."

O'Rourke inhaled nervously, then crushed his cigarette into the ashtray. "I went to Spain last year," he admitted. "This bird talked me into it." He was unwilling to admit more than that. It was nobody's business that he'd felt on edge the entire time he was in Torremolinos and knew that he'd feel equally on edge in any other place where he couldn't understand the language. "Why don't you get Trumper to do the job?"

"I suspect that the police are keeping an eye on him. And even he concedes that you're more intelligent."

True, thought O'Rourke. "I don't know," he said skeptically.

"This job requires a high level of intelligence. Cochran is a professional smuggler, a very good one. There aren't many people who are a match for him."

O'Rourke's interest revived. "Go on."

"Sometime within the next ten days or so he'll be leaving London with a large amount of money. He'll take the Sealink steamer from Harwich to the Hook of Holland and proceed from there to Geneva on the Rheingold. The money isn't his, of course, and I want it taken from him between the time he arrives in Holland and the time he arrives in Geneva."

"Why?"

"What do you mean—'why?'"

"Why can't I do it here?"

"The reason for that is confidential, between my client and myself." Garwood paused. "But I can tell you this much. The money belongs on the Continent. My client lives there."

"How did he get it over here?"

"He had it invested over here. He liquidated his investment. And shortly after that he was robbed."

O'Rourke was tempted to ask what the investment had been and how the robbery had occurred, but he decided that it didn't matter. He was being offered a job, and either he'd take it or he wouldn't. Generally, he considered lawyers a bad lot. On the other hand, you never knew when you might need one. Garwood probably talked out of both sides of his mouth, the same as the rest of them; and he had a funny way of looking at you besides—as if you were some kind of bacteria or something. But he seemed the sort who managed to keep up with things. "How do you know so much about what this American is going to do?" he asked instead.

"I've been informed."

"Ah." O'Rourke understood about informers. On occasion, when he'd deemed it necessary, he'd been one.

"You, I should think, will want to cover the route in advance, in order to determine the best means and the best place."

"To steal a suitcase full of money? That'll hardly be necessary." O'Rourke's voice was heavy with scorn. "I can do it with one hand tied behind my back."

"I'm afraid it's liable to be a bit more difficult than you think. Cochran doesn't carry the money in a suitcase."

"How—?" O'Rourke stopped abruptly. He'd heard footsteps on the stairs.

Two men came into the dining room balancing plates and cups. They seated themselves at a table some fifteen feet away.

"You know them?" O'Rourke asked in a low voice.

Garwood glanced over his shoulder. "No, but they're too far away to hear us."

Nevertheless O'Rourke kept his eye on the men and his voice down. "How does he carry it?"

"On his person."

"But—"

"In some kind of undergarment."

"Ah." O'Rourke also understood about undergarments. He himself had never dealt in heroin or any hard drug, but friends of his had done so. He reached for another cigarette. He hesitated before lighting it, however. His eyes narrowed. How could he get the money from Cochran if Cochran was riding on a train and had the money next to his skin? "I see what you mean," he said. His eyes were little more than slits as he struck a match and put it to the cigarette. "I'd have to get him off the train. I might even have to hurt him."

Garwood drank some tea. He said nothing.

There was a prolonged silence.

"How much is it worth to you?" O'Rourke said at last.

"Two thousand pounds."

"Don't make me laugh. I don't do anything for less than five."

"That isn't what I've been told. In addition to your expenses, of course."

O'Rourke's eyes flashed. He silently damned Trumper as well as Garwood. "Not when I have to go to a sodding foreign country!"

Garwood appeared to be thinking it over. "Very well. Two thousand five hundred and expenses."

"No, thank you very much. Not even as a favor to a friend." He blew a thin cloud of smoke toward the ceiling. He hoped that Garwood had noticed the bracelet and recognized the quality of the suede coat. The old bastard certainly wasn't much of a dresser himself. His suit jacket had a loose button, and the sweater he was wearing under it was unraveled at the neck.

"Three thousand. You drive a hard bargain, O'Rourke."

O'Rourke pursed his lips. "All right," he said reluctantly. "But only as a favor to a friend." He felt a surge of triumph. In the end, he would have settled for two thousand. For all his airs, the solicitor wasn't much of a negotiator.

Garwood took a white envelope from his pocket. "This contains your ticket to Geneva and three hundred pounds for your preliminary expenses. You leave tomorrow night at eight o'clock from Liverpool Street Station. We'll meet here again at the same time a week from today, and you'll tell me the plans you've made."

"What about the three thousand?"

"One half when we meet a week from today, the balance when you hand the money over to me."

Without bothering to open it, O'Rourke put the envelope into the pocket of his overcoat. He would have preferred a bit more time to get ready, but he supposed there was nothing Garwood could do about that—he was bound by Cochran's plans. "A week from today, same time." He put the cigarette between his lips and stood up. "But not here. I don't fancy this place."

"It's near my bank," Garwood said.

O'Rourke shrugged. Three thousand pounds was three thousand pounds. "As you like," he said nonchalantly. And, with a final glance at the two men who were eating their lunch, he made his way to the stairs.

Garwood gazed at the cup of coffee O'Rourke had left untouched. The conversation had been less difficult than he'd expected, and the results were gratifying. He'd been prepared to go to five thousand. Even six, if necessary.

Actually, he thought, O'Rourke was quite nice-looking. Unfortunately, however, his taste in clothes was garish. And he was a frightfully compulsive smoker.

But none of that really mattered. What mattered was that he could now believe everything he'd heard about Kenneth O'Rourke. Namely, that although he was clever enough not to get caught, he was a genuine psychopath.

4

Cochran could still remember the one and only time he'd gone to the office uninvited. Arlen had been furious.

"I never want to see you in here again unless I ask you to come," he'd hissed.

Arlen was good at hissing. He hissed even when he didn't mean to, for he habitually spoke in a low voice and he had a way of prolonging s's that made him sound more venomous than he was. But on that occasion he'd meant to, and the venom had been for real. It had made no difference to him that Cochran hadn't realized he was doing wrong, that he'd simply been passing and had decided to stop in; Cochran had broken security, and to Arlen that was unforgivable. He was obsessed by security.

By and large, Cochran thought, the obsession was a good thing. The less he knew about what Arlen did, the less contact he had with him, the better off he was. But sometimes security could be carried too far. It bothered him that he had no way of getting in touch with Arlen except through the office and Arlen even objected to his doing that. Also that he never knew where Arlen was or when he'd be back.

This was an emergency, though. Arlen had to be told about Evans.

Yet as he neared the Park Mansions Arcade he began to walk more slowly. It was most unlikely that Arlen had returned, and just as unlikely that the girl in the office would know where to reach him. As a matter of policy, Arlen changed office girls every few months. And they were no more than window dressing anyway; their duties were simply to answer inquiries from people who came in off the street and to hand out brochures. Cochran's only hope was that Arlen occasionally called in for messages. But then, since he didn't encourage messages, why would he?

At the Brompton Road entrance to the arcade, indecision brought him to a halt. After a moment, however, he turned and strode purposefully into the vaulted corridor that connected Brompton Road with Kensington Road. Right or wrong, he had to make the attempt.

Despite its location in the busiest section of Knightsbridge, and despite the fact that it was a mere stone's throw from his flat, Cochran disliked this particular piece of real estate. If he were Arlen, he would have chosen a different site for Ardmore Properties, Ltd. One that was more cheerful. As it was, Arlen's desk faced the window, and the window looked out on the dreary rotunda in the middle of the arcade. Neither indoors nor outdoors, with a broad roof of glass that seemed never to be washed and a disorderly arrangement of plants that seemed never to be dusted, the rotunda managed to make even the brightest day gloomy. But Arlen was the one who had to sit there, and Arlen didn't appear to mind.

Passing the photocopy shop and the shop that sold antique jewelry, Cochran approached the shop that dealt in dreams of palm trees and sunshine—Ardmore Properties, Ltd.

The shop was closed.

A cardboard sign that resembled a clock hung on the inside

of the door. It said, "WILL RETURN AT," and the hands pointed to one thirty.

Cochran swore.

Reluctantly he retraced his steps to Brompton Road. He had no alternate plan. No alternate destination either. He wasn't due at Garwood's office until two.

At loose ends, he strolled idly westward until he came to Montpelier Street. There he found that the Crown and Sceptre was open. He went in and ordered a half-pint of beer.

Sitting alone in the booth, he let his thoughts drift. They drifted back to his first meeting with Arlen. He'd been drinking beer in a pub then too. But a very different pub in a very different neighborhood. The Witch and Warlock, on Chepstow Road.

Stephanie had died on the fifth of December. He blamed himself for her death. Half out of his mind with grief and self-reproach, he began to walk the streets of London.

And at the end of March he was still walking.

He'd covered some two thousand miles by then, all within London. Up one street and down another, ritualistically, regardless of weather, with no goal but to keep moving, block after block, mile after mile—he walked. He wasn't consciously trying to atone, nor was he consciously trying to injure himself. Nevertheless he was, almost literally, walking himself to death. He'd lost thirty-five pounds and picked up a cough he couldn't get rid of. His skin had taken on a pasty look. His eyes were red-rimmed and bloodshot.

Yet at no point was he irrational or unaware. He always knew where he was and what he was seeing. He recognized the differences between neighborhoods, and when he found one that particularly interested him he returned to it on subsequent days. Occasionally, when his legs wouldn't carry him any farther, he went into a cinema and watched a movie until his muscles relaxed. He even rode buses and the Underground to get home from distant points. But mainly he just walked. Eight or ten hours a day. Because walking was the only activity that seemed to ease the despondency that washed over him each morning with the regularity of a tide.

Sometimes he thought about the future and worried. He couldn't return to the United States, it was impossible to get a work permit in England, and the money he'd brought with him was running out. He'd moved into an eight-by-twelve room with an iron bed and a warped chest of drawers in a small hotel on Ossington Street near Notting Hill Gate. His diet consisted of sandwiches and beer taken here and there at pubs, especially at the Witch and Warlock, which was located only a few blocks from where he lived and which was cheap. He didn't know what he was going to do when his money was gone. He realized that in any other country he would be up against the same stone wall: the work permit. There appeared to be no way for him to stave off ultimate destitution.

Having no friends, he talked to strangers. Mostly at the Witch and Warlock. He felt more comfortable there than anywhere else. Some of the strangers ignored him, others didn't. He hardly cared. It was the sound of his own voice that he needed, to prove to himself that he was still a member of the human species. Two pints of beer on an empty stomach were enough to get him started, and when he found a willing listener he manufactured rambling stories about himself in which he'd inherited money from his grandfather and set out to see the world. But willing listeners were scarce, so he often found himself sitting alone with his mug of Lager and the unbearable truth.

David Arlen was one of those who responded to his overtures. In fact, it might even have been Arlen who began the conversation. Anyway, Arlen was the first person in England to buy him a drink.

They talked for over an hour. He told Arlen how, after

inheriting this money from his grandfather, he'd said to hell with it and chucked the job he had in Philadelphia one Friday and taken off for London the very next day, just like that, and how London was merely his first stop on a trip around the world. There were bits of truth in the story—he had inherited a little money from his grandfather, and he had quit his job on a Friday—but most was fiction. Arlen paid polite attention, interrupting only once, to ask how he'd obtained a passport on such short notice, but accepted Cochran's reply that he'd already had a passport.

Then, out of the blue, Arlen said, "I could use someone like you in my business. Would you be interested?"

Cochran was astounded. "Can you get me a work permit?" he asked. Everyone else had said no.

"You won't need one."

"What business are you in?"

"Property."

With no lunch and three pints of beer in him, Cochran had tipsy visions of himself showing houses, trying to remember to call the living room the lounge, the toilet the loo, the second floor the first floor. The visions made him smile. But he wasn't too tipsy to say, "Sure."

"It isn't definite, of course," Arlen said. "Let me think about it over the weekend. Could we meet here again at this same time on Monday?"

Cochran said that that was fine with him, and a few minutes later Arlen left.

The prospect of a job elated him at first, but as the weekend progressed he became convinced that the offer had been nothing more than bar talk and that Arlen wouldn't appear on Monday—so convinced, in fact, that when Monday afternoon came he almost didn't keep the appointment himself. He was walking along Bethnal Green Road at the other end of London, and it hardly seemed worth the trouble to travel all the way back to the Witch and Warlock simply to be disappointed. But a dormant instinct for survival twitched, and at the last minute he decided to take a chance. He rode the Underground to Notting Hill Gate and walked from there to the pub.

At the entrance he all but collided with Arlen, who was hurrying toward the pub from the opposite direction.

After buying him a whiskey and soda, Arlen suggested that they have dinner together and took him by taxi to a Chinese restaurant in Soho. It was the first time in over a quarter of a year that Cochran had tasted whiskey or ridden in a taxi, and the first time in almost as long that he'd had a full meal.

Arlen expressed concern about the cough. It sounded like bronchitis, he said, and gave Cochran the name of a doctor. Then, getting down to business, he again questioned him about his passport. The job, he explained, involved traveling. Cochran assured him that he had a valid United States passport that wouldn't expire for another four and a half years. Satisfied on that score, Arlen proceeded to tell him about his company.

He was, he said, the British representative for a consortium of investors that built and sold vacation and retirement homes on the Costa del Sol. The investors were people from the United States, Canada and virtually every country in Western Europe. As were the purchasers. Since the purchasers paid for the homes in their own currencies but the construction workers got their wages in Spanish pesetas and the building materials came from all over the world, much currency conversion was necessary. This was handled by a Swiss bank. One of Arlen's responsibilities was to see that the pounds paid by the British purchasers were delivered to the Swiss bank, but he wasn't always free to go to Switzerland himself and was looking for someone trustworthy to be his courier. The courier would receive a thousand pounds per trip, plus traveling expenses.

Cochran knew immediately that there was something illegal

about the operation. Not only was the pay high in relation to the work, but anyone who wanted to transfer money from one country to another could simply write a check. He even knew where the illegality lay. Britain had strict regulations about sending pounds abroad. A person wishing to do so had to get government approval, which was often refused. There were frequently stories in the newspapers about people who'd been caught trying to move money out of the country without permission. The penalties were stiff. Arlen was looking not for a courier but for a smuggler.

Yet with no hesitation at all Cochran said he'd take the job. It was a matter of self-preservation.

Arlen tactfully advanced him a hundred pounds on the spot, "for possible medical expenses," and after dinner took him to the office, where, lest there be any doubt, he showed him pictures of the apartments and villas the company sold.

Two weeks later Cochran made his first trip from London to Geneva. With a hundred and ten thousand pounds in twenty-pound notes in the pockets of a cotton vest that he wore under three layers of clothing. He'd made the vest himself.

Disproving the statement that he wasn't always free to go to Switzerland himself, Arlen met him in Geneva on that trip—and on all subsequent trips. Arlen deposited the money.

Over the next three and a half years Cochran went to Geneva nineteen times. He now received fifteen hundred pounds per trip, had his own Swiss bank account, and had progressed in stages from Ossington Street to Knightsbridge. He wasn't rich. His income, he figured, was the equivalent of three hundred dollars a week. But he'd come a long way from the road to nowhere on which Arlen had found him.

His knowledge of Arlen had increased little with the passing of time, however. They met only before a trip, when Arlen gave him the money, and at the hotel in Geneva, where Cochran gave it back and got paid. Whatever Arlen had to say to him he said on those occasions, and what he had to say seldom went beyond instructions or advice. The instructions and advice always made sense. Never travel by air, because of security checks and the possibility of lost luggage. Always go first class and dress like a prosperous tourist. Vary your routes. Don't return from Switzerland without visiting at least one other country. Pay for everything in cash.

But he had no inkling of how or where Arlen lived and little sense of what he was like as a person. He suspected that there was Latin blood in him, perhaps that he'd even been born somewhere near the Mediterranean, because of the way he spoke and because of his coloring—he had black eyes and hair and an olive complexion. He was something of a dandy—his wardrobe was large and expensive. He made references to rare wines and appeared to admire tall, blonde women. But generally he was an enigma to Cochran—someone who'd materialized in a pub, changed his life, dealt with him for years, all without ever really identifying himself.

About the business itself Cochran felt more certain. It was essentially legitimate. The people who bought the apartments and villas got them. There was no fraud. The size of the rooms, the balconies with their views of the coastline, the communal swimming pools were all that the brochures promised. The roofs didn't collapse, and the plumbing worked. Furthermore, Ardmore was breaking no law either. The only real criminal in the set-up was the one who took the money out of England: himself.

He did occasionally wonder about the scope of the operation. Were there other offices besides the one in the Park Mansions Arcade? It was hard to believe that one office could do that much business. He'd moved two and a half million pounds out of Britain in less than four years—that represented a good many houses. Could one man have sold them all?

He didn't really care. But every now and then as he sped across Europe on one of the TEE trains with well over a hundred thousand pounds on his person he couldn't help asking himself whether all of the money was going to pay for real estate. It was conceivable that Arlen, or whoever Arlen worked for, had come up with a good way of getting money out of England for *any* purpose.

But such matters weren't within his realm. He was being paid to transport money and he was transporting it. What happened to it after it reached Geneva didn't concern him.

He supposed that Arlen wasn't the only one in the company who knew of his existence. There would almost have to be others. But Arlen was the one who'd hired him and Arlen was the one who paid him. He'd never thought about who the others might be.

Until now.

Fortified with beer and a large helping of shepherd's pie and green peas, he left the Crown and Sceptre at one twenty-five and walked back to the Park Mansions Arcade.

The sign was off the door. He went in.

Arlen's desk was unoccupied, and the two neat stacks of mail on it indicated that it had been unoccupied for several days.

At the other desk a young woman was hard at work repairing a broken fingernail. She was tall and blond. Cochran had never seen her before. Noticing him, she rose and came up to the counter, bringing the emery board with her.

"I'd like to speak with Mr. Arlen," he said.

"I'm afraid he's away at the moment," she replied. The fingernail was really bothering her. She kept frowning at it.

"Can you tell me when he'll be back?"

"I'm afraid I can't. May I help you?"

"No, this is personal. Will he be calling in?"

"I wouldn't know, I'm afraid."

"Does he usually?"

"I can't say. I'm afraid I'm rather new here. My stupid lighter—I broke my nail on it."

"I'm sorry. I'd like to leave a message for Mr. Arlen, in case he does call in."

She couldn't stand it any longer. She began to file the broken fingernail. "Certainly."

"Tell him that John Cochran wants to talk to him. Tell him to call me at home. He has my number. It's important. John Cochran. Can you remember that?"

She stopped filing long enough to give him an affronted look. "Of course I can remember."

"John Cochran," he repeated.

She nodded irritably. "I heard."

He sighed and left.

The throng of Christmas shoppers was out in full force on Brompton Road. He had a hard time getting across the street, but finally made it to the Piccadilly Line station at Sloane Street.

Descending on the ancient escalator, he told himself that he hadn't expected any more satisfaction at the office than he'd got. Nevertheless he was angry. Not so much at the girl as at Arlen.

The train clattered into the station. He found a seat. The doors closed.

Hyde Park Corner, Green Park, Piccadilly Circus, Leicester Square, Covent Garden—the train rattled along under the city, each station a reminder to Cochran that he was drawing closer to an appointment he didn't want to keep. And that, after almost four years, he still had no more independence than a fly on a piece of flypaper.

At Holborn he changed to the Central Line for the brief ride to Chancery Lane.

5

There was a slot in the door. An insert in the slot said, "ENGAGED." Cochran raised his hand to knock, but at that moment the insert moved sideways with a click and the door opened.

He found himself facing a tall old man with sharp black eyes and tufts of gray hair that were like the feathers of an aroused fowl. "Mr. Garwood?"

The lawyer opened the door wider and said, "Come in, Cochran."

Cautiously Cochran advanced into the room and looked around. His first impression was that the furnishings hadn't been changed since the first occupant had installed them, some two centuries earlier. His second was that the original occupant had had good taste. The carved oak paneling, the brass chandelier, the rows of leather-bound books with gilt embossing, even the rug, which was worn completely through in places, were handsome. The scarred old desk was the size of a double bed, and the cut-crystal whiskey decanter on the table by the window reflected the afternoon light like a huge diamond.

But the decanter was empty, and the bottle beside it bore the label of a very cheap brand of sherry. The sherry didn't go with the room. Nor did the electric hotplate on the frail table by the door.

"Sit down," Garwood said, settling himself in the big chair behind the desk. "I understand that your meeting with Peter went well."

Cochran chose a wing chair and was betrayed by it. He sank down until his knees were six inches higher than his pelvis. He moved to another chair.

"Poor Peter isn't always as articulate as he might be," Garwood went on. "One feels at times as if one has to help him express himself. But I take it he managed to explain his situation."

Cochran nodded.

"I daresay you're a bit puzzled by the matter, but really, let me assure you, it's quite simple. Peter's mother is, unfortunately, very ill. Terminally ill. Peter is anxious to live abroad after her demise, but if he has to pay the prevailing scandalously high death duties, he would not have the means to do so. Therefore it behooves him to remove his mother's money to another country. Do you take my meaning?"

Cochran noticed that the lawyer's sweater was frayed.

"Do you?" Garwood demanded.

Cochran nodded again.

"Good." Garwood's tone mellowed. "The three hundred and fifty thousand are all that remains of a fortune that was once quite vast. The family goes back to—well, I daresay you don't care about such things, but a long time. Conditions change, however, and what with taxes and one thing and another, this is all that's left."

"Does Arlen know?" Cochran asked abruptly.

"About Peter's contacting you? No. I knew he wouldn't like it, so I didn't tell him. And I don't expect you to, either. Do you take my meaning?"

Cochran remained silent.

But once more the lawyer insisted on an answer. "Do you?"

"Sure," Cochran said. "So you picked a time when you knew he'd be away."

"That I did. Now do we understand each other?"

"I understand you, but I don't think you understand me. I don't like having my arm twisted."

"Be that as it may, Cochran, you *will* do this thing for Peter, and you will *not* tell Arlen about it. Arlen considers you his personal property. I don't."

"Neither do I," Cochran said. "I don't consider myself anybody's personal property."

Garwood ignored the remark. "From the standpoint of remuneration," he said, "Arlen is a better client than the Evans family. But money isn't everything, and I've known the Evanses all my life."

"Hell," Cochran said, "according to him, you're his uncle."

"Not his blood uncle. Just an old friend of the family's who's earned the title of uncle. I feel very close to him, however. I want what's best for him."

Cochran wondered how much he could believe. The entire story sounded plausible. But the beady eyes and the imperious manner put him off. People who looked and spoke like Garwood seldom wanted what was best for anyone. "When did Arlen tell you about me?" he asked.

"It was the other way around, I'm afraid. I told him about you."

"I don't understand."

"I'm the one who recommended that he employ you."

Cochran ransacked his memory, but came up with nothing. He was positive he'd never seen Garwood before. Or heard of him, either. "But that's not possible," he said presently.

"Of course it's possible. You used to frequent a pub in Chepstow Road. I can't think of the name at the moment, but, whatever it is, you went there. And you happened to fall into conversation one day with an acquaintance of mine."

"Who?"

"That's irrelevant. You did. And I'd mentioned to him that I had a client who was looking for someone to do some confidential work. He told me about you, and I told David Arlen."

"You mean Arlen wasn't at the Witch and Warlock by accident?" Cochran was amazed.

"Definitely not. He'd been going there for days, hoping to encounter you. But after his first meeting with you he had some doubts. We spent the weekend making inquiries. In the end he decided to offer you the job."

"I'll be damned!"

"Of course," Garwood continued, "others might have done as well. But Arlen was anxious to find a replacement for Rawlings as soon as possible, and you had the basic qualifications. You were a foreigner, you had no attachments, you were obviously in need of money, and—most important of all—you were available."

"I'll be damned," Cochran said again. Then he asked, "Who was Rawlings?"

"Your predecessor. He'd been arrested at Dover attempting to take a hundred and twenty thousand pounds out of the country. Naturally, Ardmore Properties made good the losses to its customers, without their knowing, but it was an expensive experience. In any event, I suggested to Arlen that next time he should employ a foreigner. Rawlings was British and had been traveling on a British passport. I'd observed that tourists pass through our ports of entry with less scrutiny."

It was conceivable, Cochran thought. In fact, it was almost certainly true. He gazed around the room with renewed interest. It wasn't at the Witch and Warlock, or even at the restaurant in Soho, that his future had been determined, but right here, within these four walls.

Cochran gave his memory another workout. A name came to him. Alfred Trumper. There was no point in asking, however; Garwood wouldn't tell him. Instead he asked, "Are you a criminal lawyer?"

Garwood looked shocked. "Good heavens, no! I've never defended a criminal in my life, nor prosecuted one either, for that matter. I rarely enter a courtroom. I simply advise my clients on wills, investments, contracts—that sort of thing. In fact, I'm an Authorized Depository—I'm authorized to perform some of the functions of a bank for my clients— which not many solicitors can say of themselves. When my clients have problems of a marital nature or a criminal nature, I retain specialists in such matters for them. They seldom have those problems, however. Their children—well, the younger generation being what it is, their children do sometimes have them. I don't myself undertake to represent them, of course—I use someone else. I—" He broke off. A note of pride had crept into his voice. He seemed to be aware of it and to be annoyed with Cochran for having sidetracked him. "But that doesn't concern you," he concluded tersely.

Again Cochran wondered how much he could believe. And again he had to admit that all of it sounded plausible. Also, he could understand why the old man was making Evans do as much of his own dirty work as possible. People like Garwood were by disposition behind-the-scenes operators. They enjoyed making plans for others to carry out. But what kind of a lawyer was it who bragged about his aloofness from crime while arranging for his client to commit a criminal act? "No, it doesn't," he agreed. "How long a sentence did Rawlings get?"

"None. Shortly after his arrest, he had an accident. The accident was fatal."

Cochran felt a sudden chill.

"That doesn't concern you either, though," Garwood went on. "What concerns you is your own future, and Peter pointed out to you, I understand, the sort of future you'll have if you don't help him get his money to Switzerland."

"He said you'd tip off the Customs and Excise men and I'd be arrested the next time I made a trip for Arlen."

"That is correct."

"Then maybe I'll have a fatal accident too, to keep me from being brought to trial."

Garwood said nothing.

"I don't like being threatened," Cochran said. "Never did."

"You're a realist, though."

"Yes."

"So you'll make the trip. And say nothing to Arlen."

"I guess I will."

"You guess you will?"

"I will."

"That's better." Garwood opened his desk drawer. He took out an envelope. "Here are your tickets and three hundred pounds for expenses. You'll leave a week from Wednesday night for the Hook of Holland and connect there with the Rheingold the following morning. Peter will be in touch with you a day or two in advance, to arrange for turning the money over to you."

"Hold on a minute," Cochran protested. "I make my own travel arrangements."

"Not in this case," Garwood said firmly. "I've researched the matter. The Customs and Excise Department is paying particular attention to Dover at the moment. The route through Holland is the safest, and that's the one I want you to take. I want no mishaps. Do I make myself clear?"

"How do you know about Dover?"

"I make it my business to know things. Two people were arrested there the week before last."

"O.K.," Cochran said. "I'll take the Rheingold route." He

stood up and reached across the desk for the envelope.

Garwood handed it to him. "Please close the door behind you on the way out."

Cochran put the envelope in his pocket and left.

He tried to be philosophical about it. He would be doing what he always did and getting paid twice as much for it. But somehow the thought of the three thousand pounds didn't make him feel good. He didn't like the idea of going behind Arlen's back.

Walking along the sidewalk toward Bishop's Court Gate, he compared Arlen with Garwood. Arlen wasn't exactly the salt of the earth, but Arlen at least treated him somewhat as a colleague and seemed to respect his skill, whereas to Garwood he was merely a tool to be used once and discarded.

But of the two men, Garwood was apparently the one with more clout.

And whether he wanted it that way or not, Garwood was the one he was now working for.

He hoped that Arlen wouldn't call the office for messages.

6

O'Rourke opened his eyes, yawned, stretched luxuriously and looked up at his reflection in the mirrored ceiling. The covers had slid to below his navel, and the mirror presented him with a view of his smooth chest and flat belly. At the same time it showed the tousled hair, the unblemished neck and shoulders of the girl beside him. She was sleeping on her stomach, and her face was buried in the pillow. Of all the women he knew, he thought, this one, Gillian, was the most satisfactory.

He took a cigarette from the packet on the bedside table and lit it. The night's activity had been strenuous, and he'd slept for only three hours, but he felt rested and comfortable.

Gradually he became aware of the sound of running water. It was coming from the bathroom. He sighed. It *had* been a good night. Drawing the covers up to his armpits, he continued to smoke and to study himself upside down in the mirror.

Gillian stirred, murmured and pulled at the blanket in her

sleep. He ran a finger across her shoulders and watched himself doing it. She murmured again.

Suddenly he remembered that he was going to have to leave London. His feeling of well-being left him. He reached for his wristwatch and looked at it. Eight thirty. In twelve hours he would be on the train, passing through the suburbs.

He began to imagine what it would be like.

The door opened, and Trumper came out of the bathroom. He was naked. Seeing that O'Rourke was awake, and ignoring the fact that Gillian was asleep, he exclaimed, "Jesus Bloody Christ, it's cold in here!"

"Don't seem so to me," O'Rourke said.

Trumper searched in the pile of clothing on the floor and found his underpants. "I feel like I've been hit by a car," he said. "I'm sore all over."

"You've no stamina," O'Rourke said. He watched Trumper pull the underpants up his legs. Good body, he thought, but beginning to get fat. Going to have to start slimming.

"Trouble is, you've too much stamina," Trumper replied. He rummaged through the clothes, found his trousers and put them on.

Gillian turned onto her side and made a complaining sound. O'Rourke frowned at her, then decided to forgive her and smiled.

"Where's my other sock?" Trumper asked, holding up a single one.

"How should I know? I'm not wearing it."

Trumper located the missing sock and leaned against the mirrored wall as he drew the sock over his foot.

Gillian woke, nestled against O'Rourke, and said, "Mmm."

O'Rourke absentmindedly patted her head, then threw back the covers and got out of bed. He went over to Trumper and said in a low voice, "Want to talk to you, mate."

"Wait till I get my shirt on."

O'Rourke inspected himself in the mirror, which ran the

full width of the room. Satisfied with the front view, he turned, folded his hands behind his head and inspected himself from the side.

Sleek, he thought. Decidedly sleek.

Trumper tucked in his shirt and bent over to look for his necktie. O'Rourke swatted him on the backside. "You're getting fat, mate."

"Can't find my bloody tie," Trumper complained.

"It's in the lounge, with your shoes, stupid."

Trumper straightened up and rubbed the spot where he'd been hit. O'Rourke took him firmly by the arm and led him into the lounge, closing the door behind them.

Trumper saw his necktie draped over the arm of a chair. "You're right," he said, and started for it.

O'Rourke tightened his grip on Trumper's arm and pulled him back. "I'm going to need some stuff," he said.

"Ouch," said Trumper. "You're hurting me." Then his eyes widened. "Some stuff? I'm clean now, Ken. You know that."

"Not hard stuff. A sleeping drug. Anesthetic, like."

"What for?"

"For this job you got me with Garwood."

Trumper eyed him suspiciously. "I don't know. Let go my arm, Ken."

O'Rourke released Trumper's arm and crushed the cigarette into an ashtray. "It's not a pill," he said. "It gets injected. It'll put this chap to sleep for a while."

"I don't want to know about it," Trumper said quickly.

O'Rourke's hand again closed around Trumper's arm. His fingers dug into the flesh. Trumper winced and turned pale.

"What do you mean you don't want to know?" O'Rourke said angrily. "I've just told you. It's for this job with Garwood. He wants it. I want it. You get it. It's from America. Called Thiopental. They use it in hospitals. Understand?"

"Please, Ken, let go."

"Understand?"

"All right, all right, I'll get it. Let go."

"One hundred milligrams," O'Rourke said, and opened his hand.

Massaging his arm, Trumper went quickly over to the chair and stepped into his shoes. He didn't bother with the tie—merely shoved it into his pocket. "What did I do with my jacket?" he asked plaintively.

"It's in the cupboard by the door," O'Rourke said.

Trumper looked at him. Stark naked, his hands at his sides, an appreciative smile on his lips, O'Rourke returned the gaze and said, "You're a lovely man."

Trumper grinned nervously and went toward the cupboard. O'Rourke stepped in front of him. "By Saturday, Trump. I'll want to see you on Saturday. Have the stuff ready by then. I don't care if you have to go to New York for it. Understand?"

"Sure, Ken, sure."

O'Rourke put his arms around him and kissed him on the cheek. "Thank you," he said.

Trumper got his jacket and left.

O'Rourke returned to the bedroom.

Gillian was fully awake now. She was reclining against the pillows, smoking one of O'Rourke's cigarettes.

He got into bed beside her, took the cigarette from between her fingers and began to smoke it himself. "Have a good sleep?" he asked.

"Not long enough," she replied. "I'd like some coffee."

"Get up and make some, then."

"I don't want it so badly as that."

"Then shut up." He put out the cigarette and began to stroke her breasts.

"Not now, Ken. Let's have some coffee first."

He ran one hand down her side and along her thigh. "Stop complaining, and roll over."

"Not yet. I'm still tired."

He slid his hand under her and gave her a hard pinch on the buttock.

She yelped. "That was cruel!"

He stroked the area he'd pinched.

She began to relax. "You're terrible," she said.

He drew her closer and eased himself onto her. Locking his arms around her, he began to rotate his hips.

She heaved a sigh of resignation and put her mouth to his.

7

Arlen always delivered the money in clear plastic envelopes, as it was packaged by the Bank of England. Each envelope contained fifty banknotes of twenty-pounds denomination.

The vest resembled a life jacket. It had thirty pockets, each large enough to hold three envelopes easily, four when stretched. Fully packed, it added between three and four inches to Cochran's girth from his armpits to his waist.

But a hundred and twenty envelopes were the maximum. And that was the problem.

Sitting cross-legged on the bed, the vest on his lap, Cochran considered alternatives. He'd considered alternatives in the past, too. He'd never come up with one that was satisfactory, however. Except, of course, to carry the money in a suitcase.

It would have been easy if banknotes of a larger denomination were available in England, but unfortunately they weren't.

It would have been easy, also, if he were willing to add more to his girth. However, Arlen had warned him, and he knew from his own experience, that customs men were trained to look for people who appeared to be out of proportion in some part of the body. Any person who aroused their curiosity in that manner was apt to receive a seemingly accidental bump, with possible dire consequences.

Once, as an experiment, Cochran had made himself a pair of long underpants with pockets like the vest. He'd never attempted to wear them, though, for the chance was too great that some of the money might fall out of a pocket and slide down his leg. With the vest, that couldn't happen. Anything that fell out of it was automatically caught by his shirt and belt.

He'd arrived at the finished product by a process of trial and error. He'd remembered the vests worn by smugglers of heroin, hashish and Swiss watch movements, and adapted the design. Although it was more suitable for items worth more per cubic inch than money, it worked for money too. But only for a certain amount.

Now he was going to have to carry almost three times that amount, and the damn thing simply wouldn't hold it.

After a while he got off the bed, took *The Times* and began cutting the pages into rectangles the size of twenty-pound notes. When he had fifty, he arranged them in a stack, took his electric iron from the cabinet and carefully ironed it. It became thinner by half. He tried it in one of the pockets. It was still too thick.

He sat down on the side of the bed and pondered.

He was still pondering when the telephone rang.

Arlen? he thought, and felt a momentary panic. He decided not to answer.

But the telephone kept ringing, and eventually he lifted it from its cradle. He would simply have to invent a story.

It wasn't Arlen at the other end of the line, however. It was Kitty Humphries.

"Ruth has arrived," she announced happily. "You must come to dinner tonight."

8

The taxi driver pocketed the fifty pence, said, "Ta," and drove off.

Humming, O'Rourke carried his suitcase into the station and paused at the bookstall to look around. He was in no hurry. He'd purposely allowed extra time, to study the layout. It might not be practical to follow Cochran from his home, in which case this was where he'd have to pick him up.

He noticed the sign over the barrier for Platform Nine: "20:00 'THE HOOK CONTINENTAL' Harwich Parkeston Quay for Holland, Germany, Scandinavia, Poland, Switzerland, Austria, Italy. Refreshment Car." The train was not yet at the platform.

He glanced at his watch. Seven twenty.

Proceeding to the cigarette-and-sweet kiosk, he paused again. The station wasn't crowded. But that didn't mean it wouldn't be crowded on the night Cochran left. A breakdown, frozen switches—anything could cause delays and cancellations. Then the station would be jammed with stranded commuters, and it would be difficult, if not impossible, to pick one man out of the crowd.

Refreshment car, he thought. Would Cochran eat on the train, at the station or before he left home?

O'Rourke walked to the entrance to the station buffet. The place didn't look appealing to him. It might appeal to Cochran, however. He couldn't guess at Cochran's tastes.

Continuing, he passed a row of barriers and presently came to an archway. Strolling through it, he found himself back at the entrance where he'd got out of the taxi. To his left was a stairway to the Liverpool Street Underground station.

Definitely a bad set-up, he thought as he retraced his steps to the kiosk. There he paused once more and made a mental outline. The gates were arranged along the short legs of a Z. But the upright line of the Z, instead of being slanted, was straight. He'd done one leg. Now he set out to do the other.

It was even worse. At the top of the Z was a tunnel. It too led to the Underground. Furthermore, he discovered as he followed it, it crossed another tunnel.

Bloody ridiculous, he thought.

Returning the way he'd come, he detoured to the ticket office and went up to one of the windows. "The Hook Continental," he asked, "does it make any stops between here and Harwich?"

The clerk said that it didn't.

O'Rourke left the ticket office and gave his attention to the overhead bridge. Climbing the steps, he walked from one end of the bridge to the other. It was merely a shortcut to the farthest platforms and was of no use to him. Too difficult to identify someone from fifteen feet in the air. And the bar, which was called the Europa Bistro and was located at the level of the bridge, almost directly above Platform Nine, was unsatisfactory for the same reason.

Descending the stairs to the level of the trains, he seated himself on one of the benches facing the track for the Hook Continental. If for any reason he was unable to follow Cochran from his house, the only place he could be sure of spotting him was at the barrier.

But while he was sitting there, even that certainty disappeared, for at twenty minutes to eight the train backed into position, and O'Rourke realized that it wasn't necessary to go through the barrier to board the train; the first-class coaches stopped directly in front of where he was sitting. All he had to do was walk a few yards and climb aboard. And Cochran would be able to do the same.

Nevertheless, he decided he had little to worry about. There would be plenty of opportunities to pick up Cochran's trail later. On the train, boarding the ship, at the pier in Holland. What he was doing now was almost unnecessary. Only Kenneth O'Rourke would think of the possibility that his man might change his mind at the last minute and take a different route. Kenneth O'Rourke thought of everything.

At ten minutes to eight he entered the train. Three people were already seated in his compartment—an elderly man, an elderly woman and a younger woman who, in slacks, turtleneck sweater and rubber-soled shoes, looked like a man. He treated all of them to a friendly smile, hoisted his suitcase onto the overhead rack and took his seat. "Nice evening," he said.

His three fellow travelers agreed that it was.

Satisfied that they spoke English, he settled back and lit a cigarette.

Just before the train pulled out, the fifth occupant of the compartment arrived, a young woman, and took the seat opposite his. This irritated him, because it meant he couldn't put his feet up, but since she wasn't bad-looking he was willing to overlook the inconvenience, and within minutes of their departure he fell into conversation with her. She was from Oxford, she said, and she was on her way to Amsterdam, where she was meeting a friend. She and her friend were then going to Klosters for a week's skiing.

O'Rourke told her that he was an economist who was being summoned to Geneva for consultation by one of the Swiss banks. She seemed to find that exciting, and the conversation lasted for some time.

But in the end it was the other three passengers who set his imagination off. For while they were reluctant to talk to him, for some reason, they were willing enough to talk to the young woman from Oxford.

All three of them, he learned, were traveling together. The woman in slacks was the daughter of the elderly man, but the elderly woman wasn't her mother—merely her father's landlady. The two old people were, O'Rourke concluded, lovers, and he was both amused and repelled by the thought of them in bed together. The old lady was fat and bowlegged, and the old man had blue veins that showed through the skin of his hands and somehow reminded O'Rourke of a road map.

They were en route to The Hague to spend Christmas with the younger woman's son, who taught in a school there. He was driving to the Hook of Holland to meet them. Upon hearing this, the young woman from Oxford said that he'd have to get up awfully early in order to be at the dock when the steamer arrived, and the teacher's mother agreed. However, she added, there was a comfortable buffet in the terminal where they could wait if he was late.

O'Rourke had already thought about cars. Now, as the train sped across Essex toward the North Sea, he began to think about terminals. He pictured a large warehouse filled with crates and forklifts, perhaps even metal containers.

After a while, he took an exploratory walk through the train. The refreshment car and the second-class coaches beyond it were crowded with people whose looks he didn't like—undistinguished types who didn't know how to dress properly—and he returned to his own compartment as quickly as possible. But he'd convinced himself that if he missed Cochran at the station it would be easy to find him on the train.

From time to time he looked out the window. The night was very dark, though; all he could see, aside from the reflections of the four other passengers in the compartment and himself, were the lights of automobiles on the highway that paralleled the railroad tracks. Occasionally he noted a large green directional sign illuminated by clusters of orange fog lamps, and wondered whether the highways on the Continent were as well marked as those in England. He doubted that they were.

Parkeston Quay wasn't what he'd expected it to be. The terminal was smaller, brighter and more modern than anything he remembered seeing along the Thames in London.

He hoped that the terminal in Holland was different.

He stood to one side and let the second-class passengers push their way toward the passport-control desks—as such people would. When the crowd had thinned, he took his place in queue. The formalities were minimal. The passport-control officer took his embarkation card and stamped his passport with hardly a glance at him, and he proceeded through the customs area, suitcase in hand, without being questioned. He could understand why someone smuggling money out of the country would choose this route.

At the foot of the escalator he saw a sign that said, "KONINGIN JULIANA, HOEK VAN HOLLAND," and he had a moment's apprehension. The damn foreign talk was starting already. You'd think that in England at least they'd say it in English. But he stepped onto the escalator, rode to the upper level of the terminal and followed the crowd along the ramp to the gangplank. There he hesitated again. He had to remind himself that he was Kenneth O'Rourke and Kenneth

O'Rourke feared nothing. Once he'd done that, however, he crossed the gangplank jauntily.

A stewardess took his ticket, directed him to his cabin and asked him whether he'd prefer coffee, tea or orange juice in the morning.

"Coffee, love," he said, and went off down the passageway.

The cabin was an outrage. A prison cell was larger. The bed was only two feet wide. There was no toilet. He'd have to speak to Garwood about that. Next time he wanted better accommodations.

Oppressed by the cabin, he returned to the stairwell, climbed two flights and found the bar. All the stools were occupied, and people were standing. He elbowed his way up to the counter. The bartender was blond and blue-eyed and reminded him of Trumper. But his haircut and the fact that he spoke Dutch to some of the passengers marked him as coming from Holland and being therefore even more slow-witted than Trumper. O'Rourke waited to be noticed. After an annoyingly long time, he was.

"Whiskey and soda," he said slowly and distinctly, as if to a child.

The bartender made the drink and served it. "Three guilders twenty-five," he said.

"I'm English," O'Rourke said, putting down a five-pound note.

The bartender shrugged, took the money and gave him change in guilders.

O'Rourke studied the change before putting it in his pocket. He had a feeling that he'd been cheated, but he wasn't sure.

A blast of the ship's whistle made him jump.

He drank his whiskey and soda quickly and ordered another. When he'd finished the second, he went out on deck.

A cold wind tore at his coat and did damage to the arrangement of his hair. Leaning into the wind, he went to the rail. The lights of Harwich were a faint glow in the distance.

There was no moon. A narrow swath of foam was visible as it broke away from the ship, but beyond that everything was black. The only other creature in sight was a seagull perched on the rail.

On the ship it would be a piece of cake, O'Rourke thought. An obscure corner of a deserted deck. A single blow to the back of the head. A quick stripping of the body, then overboard with it. A minute and a half in all. And seagulls made poor witnesses.

But Garwood didn't want it done on the ship, and O'Rourke could understand why. Customs inspection in Holland.

He sighed regretfully and returned to the shelter of the ship's interior. After pausing in front of a mirror to put his hair in order, he went down to the reception foyer to ask where he could convert some money. An officer at the Purser's counter directed him to the Change.

He took his place in the queue. Ahead of him was the young woman from Oxford. He tapped her on the shoulder. She turned around and smiled.

"Bloody bother, changing money, isn't it?" he said.

"There wasn't time in London," she said.

"Would you care for a drink?"

"I wouldn't mind."

They completed their transactions and found a table in the bar. The young woman ordered a gin and tonic, and O'Rourke another whiskey and soda. She really was rather attractive, he thought. A bit bony perhaps, but all in all not bad.

"The only thing I don't like about my work," he said, "is the amount of traveling I have to do. Switzerland this week, France the week after Christmas, then the United States for a month. I might as well not have a home, for all I'm in it."

"I wish I could travel more," she said.

"To each his own." He lit another cigarette and moved his leg until it touched hers. "I started out to become an artist. Was rather good at it, actually. Oils, mostly. But my father wanted me to go into business. More substantial, he said. You know how it is with families. Always advising you."

The waiter brought their drinks.

"I know," the young woman said. If she was aware of O'Rourke's leg against hers, she gave no sign of it.

O'Rourke put his arm on the table, so that she could see the gold bracelet. "Of course," he went on, "everything has its rewards, and I do enjoy my comforts. The perks, you know. Quite substantial, in my position. I mean, a person has to have something, and with the bloody taxes, what else is there?"

"Where are you going to stay in Switzerland?" she asked.

"I haven't decided." He hoped that she could tell the difference between fourteen-karat gold and imitation. "I get bored staying in the same hotel all the time."

"I suppose you would."

He removed his hand from the table, dropped it into his lap, then slid it over until it was resting on her knee.

She gave him a startled glance, but said nothing.

"Funny old couple on the train, weren't they? An old man and an old lady like that, making it—hardly seems decent, does it?" He began to run his hand along the inside of her leg.

She blushed and moved her leg. "I really must be going," she said. "We have to get up early."

"Come on now, love. It's not even midnight." He reached for her leg again.

"No, really." She started to get up. "Thank you for the drink."

"If there's anything I hate," he said angrily, "it's a bloody tease."

She grabbed her handbag and hurried from the table.

"Bitch," he said under his breath. In England he would have gone after her and told her a thing or two, but here he restrained himself.

He crushed out his cigarette and gulped his drink. His fury diminished. He had more important things to think about than skinny whores who took advantage. He had plans to make. This wasn't a holiday.

He withdrew into himself and began to concentrate. The steps he'd taken so far seemed adequate. But one had to consider every possibility.

9

"I've become an emotional cripple," Cochran had once told Kitty. "I've become incapable of loving anyone."

"That's not true," she'd protested. "You're simply gun-shy. You don't want to be hurt again. I daresay you'll get over it when you meet the right person."

He hadn't believed her.

And he still didn't believe her. There was no right person. Not for him.

With Kitty, he'd tried. And she'd done all she could to make it easy for him. They'd been two lonely people, in need. They'd been able to give each other something. But what he'd given wasn't love, and both of them had known it. He'd helped her through the early months of her widowhood with his company, with his body. But the inhibiting force that kept him from delivering himself completely to anyone else had also kept him from delivering himself completely to Kitty.

Now she was remarried. Happily. To Ian Humphries. And

both of them were Cochran's friends, the only close friends he had in England.

He was glad that he and Kitty had faced the truth. He wished, however, that the truth had been different.

As for Ruth Watts, he knew nothing about her. All he knew was that Kitty had asked him to meet her and be nice to her because she was a friend of Cora Douglas, "And Cora was nice to me when I was in the States.

"You needn't feel that you have to," Kitty had added, "but I imagine she'd enjoy spending an afternoon or evening with someone besides Ian and me, and she doesn't know anyone else in London."

Being nice meant lunch or dinner and maybe a play. And he'd agreed.

But now, as he walked the short distance to the Humphries flat, he was sorry that he had. He was in no mood to be nice to anyone. Evans, Garwood, Arlen, the money—he was worried.

Furthermore, much as he liked Kitty and Ian, he sometimes felt uncomfortable when he visited them. Kitty had occupied the flat on Hans Place with her first husband. Now she was occupying it with her second. But for some months in between she'd occupied it with Cochran. He'd never lived there full time, but he'd spent far more nights there, during those months, than he'd spent at his own place.

The first husband didn't bother him—he hadn't known him. But it did occasionally disturb him to walk into the bathroom and see Ian's shaving gear on the shelf where his own had stood, to find Ian's raincoat on that peg of the clothes tree that had once been reserved for his.

It was his own fault that he'd gone from lover to friend of the family, and he accepted his reduced status without rancor. Even if he'd been in love with Kitty, he couldn't have married her. Yet the little reminders of Ian's permanent tenancy in the flat, and in Kitty's life, made him all the more aware of his own shortcomings and of the fact that there was a hole in his existence—one that could never be patched.

Wonderful aromas wrapped themselves around him as he walked into the hall. Kitty was an expert cook and evidently she was going all out tonight.

She kissed him, then said in a low voice, "She's a teacher."

He made a face. "That's all I need."

She turned on a smile and took his arm.

He turned on a matching smile and let himself be led into the lounge.

While Kitty made the introductions, Ian poured him a whiskey. He accepted it gratefully. He had the feeling that he was going to need more than one.

And he was right. He needed three.

Even Ian, who habitually drank sherry before dinner, seemed to be feeling the need for something stronger. He downed the biggest shot of Scotch Cochran had ever seen him consume. And Kitty, who usually handled the cooking with great aplomb, kept popping in and out of the kitchen with an anxious frown.

It wasn't, Cochran decided after a while, that the American woman was socially inept. It was simply that she was bewildered. She'd been in England for less than twelve hours. It was the first time she'd been outside the United States. And she was among people she'd been assured she was going to adore. But she couldn't think of anything to say to them and was painfully aware that they couldn't think of anything to say to her. In addition, the poor thing wasn't used to the temperature of an English home in December and was obviously cold. She kept rubbing her hands and hugging herself, but was too polite to complain. He felt sorry for her, but didn't know what to do about it. To suggest that she borrow one of Kitty's sweaters would probably add to her embarrassment.

At the same time, he appreciated the gallant effort that

Ian and Kitty were making. He knew that for the sake of the Watts woman they wished they could make the room warmer, but the central heating was already turned up as high as it would go. He sensed that although both of them were normally lively talkers, they were somehow at a loss with this particular guest.

He made an effort, too. But he was no more successful than the other three.

Ian poured the wine as soon as they were seated in the dining room. Even before Kitty brought out the first course. And drank half a glass without pausing for breath. And for a moment turned beet red.

Kitty served the prawns and sat down.

There was another awkward silence.

Cochran, feeling the drinks he'd had, came to the conclusion that the trouble was everyone was being too polite. Turning to the Watts woman, he said, "It beats me what the hell you're doing over here anyway."

She gave him a startled look.

"I mean it," he went on. "I mean, a single woman, a schoolteacher, alone, coming to England this time of year when she ought to be home with her family—what the hell for? What do you expect to find over here that you haven't got at home?"

"John!" Kitty said sharply. She turned to Ruth. "What John means—" she began soothingly.

"I know what he means," Ruth said. She eyed him. "What disturbs you—that I'm a woman, a schoolteacher or alone?" Her face had gone pink, but some of the self-consciousness had disappeared.

"All three. None. I don't know." He drank some wine and suddenly felt lightheaded. "I mean, Kitty and Ian belong here—it's their country. And I have to be here—it's where I live. But you—this is a hell of a time of year to be off in a strange place by yourself."

"You're being rude," Kitty told him.

"No," Ruth said. "I understand. It's not the fact that I'm over here alone that bothers him, but the fact that *he* is." Once more she eyed him, this time with a smile. "In a way, you're right. It does seem strange, my being here, even to me. But, you see, I have no family, so I'm really no worse off over here than I would be at home, and since I'm supposed to take over the apartment in Munich on January first, I thought I might as well leave before Christmas and see a few sights along the way." She'd already explained haltingly before dinner that she was going to Germany to study for a year and that she was exchanging apartments with a German woman. She turned back to Kitty. "The shrimps are delicious."

"Thank you," said Kitty. "You'll enjoy Munich, I'm sure. It's quite picturesque. But you haven't told us what it is you're going there to study."

"The Wittelsbachs," Ruth said.

Ian put down his fork. "What are those, might I ask?"

"The Wittelsbach family. The Electors of Bavaria. That's the subject of my dissertation."

"How fascinating," Kitty said, without much conviction.

"Well, really, they are," Ruth said. " 'The Electors of Bavaria: The Uses and Abuses of Power'—that's my title. It sounds rather esoteric, I know, but doctoral dissertations have to. That's the way the game is played."

Cochran finished his prawns. "The Electors of Bavaria," he said, shaking his head.

Ruth glanced at him, then said to Kitty, "The Wittelsbachs ruled longer than any family in Europe. The Tudors, the Stuarts, the Bourbons, the Romanovs, the Hapsburgs—they came and went; but the Wittelsbachs stayed in power. For seven hundred and fifty years. And became, in the process, one of the richest families in the world. It's rather remarkable, when you stop to consider. So many changes took place during that time, yet somehow the Wittelsbachs managed to cope with all of them. We can learn something from that, I think."

"What?" Cochran asked. "What can we learn?"

"To roll with the punches," she replied.

He laughed.

Kitty looked relieved. The ice had been broken. She refused Ruth's offer of help and cleared the table herself, then brought out the roast.

Ian refilled the wineglasses.

Ruth, having at last started to talk, now seemed unable to stop. She went on about the various Maximilians and Lola Montez and Mad King Ludwig, who, she was convinced, hadn't been really mad but merely neurotic and who had been murdered because in a few years he'd spent most of the money it had taken his forebears seven centuries to accumulate, and that was the thing about the Wittelsbachs—they were practical; when some member of the family got out of line, the others dealt with him, although of course they didn't usually resort to murder; and anyway, no one would ever really know whether it was murder or suicide. That is, they couldn't prove it.

Cochran kept his mouth shut. He made no attempt to concentrate on what Ruth was saying. Instead, he concentrated on her face. It was flushed now, either from the wine or from some inner excitement. Her present animation, he thought, was part of the same self-consciousness that had made her so uncommunicative before, and he couldn't see what she had to be self-conscious about. She was attractive enough. Bright enough too, apparently.

Kitty cleared the table again and brought out the apple tarts.

Ian, sated with food and wine, was wearing an expression of supreme contentment. His wife had done him proud.

Cochran had a moment of intense melancholy.

"What's the matter?" Ruth asked.

"The matter?"

"You looked so sad just then."

"Nothing's the matter," he said irritably.

"You said you have to live here," she reminded him. "Is that on account of your work?"

"I don't work. I'm retired."

"Then—?"

"Because I do, that's all."

Kitty tactfully changed the subject, and presently they returned to the lounge for coffee.

But Cochran was sober now, and he couldn't shake off the depression that had suddenly descended on him. While the others talked, he sat in silence, lost in his own dark thoughts, aware that he was having the same bad effect on the group after dinner that Ruth had had on it before, yet unable to rouse himself.

Ian offered him a glass of port.

He declined.

And at ten thirty he announced that he'd better be getting home.

"Me too," Ruth said quickly. "I'm still on American time, and everything seems peculiar."

"But it's early," Kitty protested halfheartedly.

"It'll take me a few days to adjust, I'm afraid," Ruth said.

"John will see you to your hotel," Kitty told her.

"Sure," he said without enthusiasm.

"It isn't necessary," Ruth said. "My hotel is only five minutes from here."

"He's going that way," Kitty insisted. "Ruth is staying at the Basil Street Hotel," she explained to Cochran.

Cochran looked at her. The Basil Street Hotel was less than two hundred feet from where he lived. He wondered whether the fact that Ruth was staying there was pure coincidence. He decided that it was. "Sure," he said again.

They got their coats and after a leavetaking that was excessively polite on everyone's part they went down to the street.

They walked in silence along the little garden square. There was no moon. The air was cold. Cochran was still depressed.

"You don't like personal questions, do you?" Ruth asked presently.

He glanced at her and missed a step, but caught up. "Not particularly."

They continued for some distance without saying anything further. Then Ruth spoke again. "I'm sorry I spoiled your evening."

This remark, too, caused him to miss a step. "You didn't." It didn't sound convincing, even to him.

"It's all so strange, you see."

"Being in England?"

"Being on my own."

"You're not used to it?"

"No."

He waited for her to elaborate, but she didn't.

They turned the corner into Hans Road.

"Maybe Holland will be different," she said at last. "There I'm staying with a friend."

"You're going to Holland too?"

"On Monday. That's where I'll be for Christmas."

He guided her into Basil Street, and as they strolled toward the hotel she explained that Beatrix Coertsen, the friend with whom she would stay in Holland, was a professor of history at the University of Amsterdam. They'd become acquainted during the year Beatrix had taught at the University of Chicago, where Ruth had been studying. Beatrix was one of the world's leading authorities on the Franco-Prussian War, and of course it was the Franco-Prussian War that had set the stage for World War I and all that followed.

Cochran, whose interest in the Franco-Prussian War was less than consuming, interrupted her to point out the building in which he lived, and after that she remained silent.

She was a strange woman, he thought.

They reached the entrance to the hotel, and she thanked him for walking her home. He recalled the promise he'd made to Kitty, and decided to renege: another two hours of the Electors of Bavaria would be more than he could handle.

"It's been nice meeting you," he said. "Good luck with your research."

They shook hands, and she went into the hotel.

Like the middle of the night, O'Rourke thought.

He stood for a few minutes near the foot of the gangplank, watching the passengers disembark. They were a sleepy and disheveled group. Most were carrying suitcases and parcels, but a few, having consigned their luggage to the porters on the ship for delivery somewhere inside the terminal, were merely rubbing their eyes and trying to come fully awake. At Harwich everyone had trooped through passport control and boarded the ship in a steady stream, but here it was different—they straggled ashore in clusters, with no air of urgency.

He'd learned that it was an hour later in Holland than it was in England and he'd adjusted his watch. Now he consulted it. Six twenty-five.

But like the middle of the night. A very dark night, at that. No moon. Only one star. And a certain stillness over everything.

The ship was lighted. So was the inside of the terminal. The no-man's-land between was like a quiet street at midnight, however. Two or three dockworkers moved about silently. Only two or three.

The air was bitterly cold, and presently O'Rourke carried his suitcase into the terminal. The hush that prevailed outside the building also prevailed inside. A handful of people stood in a queue at each of the passport-control desks and were quickly processed. He joined the longest of the queues, in order to give himself time to observe, but the people ahead of him had their passports stamped without delay, and so did he. In less than two minutes he was putting his passport back into his pocket and walking into the customs area.

He stopped to look around, and was disappointed. The terminal wasn't what he'd hoped for. It had nothing in common with a warehouse. It was more like the railway station at Reading. Larger perhaps, and cleaner, but the same sort of place.

Half a dozen passengers were milling about, collecting baggage which had been brought to that point by porters from the ship, turning it over to other porters to be taken to the trains. No noise, no crowding, no fuss.

Unsuitable, he thought.

The customs inspectors made no attempt to examine his suitcase, and he left the area. A dimly lit corridor with a Change on one side and a ticket office on the other led to the exit. He followed it, opened the door and paused outside to get his bearings, then turned to his left and began a careful tour of inspection.

He noted that he was on Platform 3B. On one side of the platform stood the boat train to Amsterdam. On the other side was the terminal building, with a sign indicating the entrance to the buffet. He detoured and entered the buffet. It was large, dingy and relatively empty. A few railway employees in uniform sat at one of the long tables, drinking coffee, and a couple dozen of the ship's passengers were breakfasting before continuing on to wherever they were going. That was all. Suddenly he drew a sharp breath. Among the diners he saw the trio who had shared his compartment from London to Harwich, and with them was the young woman from Oxford. He guessed that she was telling them about him. He was tempted to go over to her and give her a piece of his mind, but he resisted the temptation and quickly left the building.

Beyond the end of the platform was a car-park. It was almost filled with cars. A lone taxi waited at the corner nearest the terminal. The driver of the taxi appeared to be asleep.

O'Rourke retraced his steps, and went to the opposite end of the terminal. Here he found three other trains. The signs that identified them showed that they were due to depart within minutes of one another. The Rheingold, 7:17. The Rhein Express, 7:33. The Holland-Scandinavië Express, 7:36.

He boarded the Rheingold, found his compartment, put his suitcase on the rack and got off again. From the platform he could see into the train on each side. The Rhein Express was crowded, the Rheingold wasn't. And at the moment there was no one on the platform.

Presently a man appeared, evidently having just come from the customs area. He approached O'Rourke, listing from the weight of a large suitcase he was carrying, passed him and entered the Rheingold at the next coach. Once more there was no one on the platform.

O'Rourke let himself imagine that the man had been Cochran.

Deep in thought, he walked back toward the terminal. It puzzled him that with hundreds of people leaving the ship and distributing themselves among five trains there was so little activity. He concluded that it was because there was such a time lapse between the docking of the ship and the departures of the trains. But he wondered whether things were always as quiet as they were now.

Between the terminal building and the three trains that

were leaving for Germany were a wide service corridor and some outbuildings. He investigated. Through an open doorway he saw a man seated at a desk in one of the outbuildings, filling out a form. The man was alone. Against the outside wall of the little structure was a bicycle rack. Evidently some of the employees bicycled to work; and if so, most of them hadn't yet showed up, for the rack had only one bicycle in it.

The service corridor led from the railway platforms to the freight yard, which was enclosed by a fence. Two carts loaded with mailbags stood near the gate in the fence. They were unattended. O'Rourke skirted them and strolled at a leisurely pace toward the gate. It was open, and there was no one in the guard's shed.

Complacent, he thought.

He entered the restricted area. No one was about, and there were few lights. He glanced up at the sky. The one star that had been shining before was still shining. Again he had the feeling that it was like the middle of the night.

Deciding not to push his luck, he left the freight yard and ambled back along the platform between the Rhein Express and the Rheingold. At the far end he discerned a dark shape and he kept going until he came to it. It was a small brick building that extended across almost the entire width of the platform. A sign identified it as a water closet. It was unlocked. He went inside. In addition to the urinals and washbasins were two booths with wooden doors. These too were unlocked. He guessed that the facility was intended mostly for railway personnel and that it was seldom used.

He left the building, proceeded along the Rheingold until he reached his coach, and went aboard.

He was the only passenger in the compartment.

He lit a cigarette.

Not impossible, he thought.

Five minutes later, the train glided out of the terminal.

II

Shortly after the train left Koblenz, O'Rourke went into the restaurant car. He was thoroughly bored by then and glad to have something to do. He'd smoked an entire packet of cigarettes; been annoyed by all the foreigners who got on the train at one city and off at the next; been outraged by the Dutch train attendant who had taken his ticket but couldn't understand a simple question put to him in English; and nursed a deep resentment of the German official who had scrutinized him for a full minute while checking his passport at Emmerich. Evidently a lot of spies traveled on this particular train, and nobody trusted anybody.

As he ate his meal he looked out the window. The tracks were running parallel to the Rhein. The river, even in winter, was like a bloody motorway. Low-slung barges were almost as numerous as Morris Minis on the M-4, and there were dozens of other types of craft as well. The hills on both sides of the river were steep and were planted with symmetrical rows of grapevines. There seemed to be hardly any ground that wasn't being put to some use, and he decided that the Rhein valley was like the country the train had passed through farther north: congested.

An occasional ruin caught his eye. An old castle or monastery perched hundreds of feet up the side of a slope, ideally situated for the occupants to blast the hell out of anyone who tried to get up the slope without an invitation. Things hadn't changed much. The nobility and the bloody priests always knew how to look after themselves. Always. Because they were cleverer than anyone else. It paid to be clever.

He was finishing his wine when the train drew into Mainz. As at the other stations, there was a crowd getting on the train, a crowd getting off, and little enough time for either group. The train stopped for only two or three minutes at each city. But it made more stops than he'd imagined it would. Schiedam-Rotterdam West, Utrecht, Arnhem, Emmerich, Duisburg, Düsseldorf, Köln, Bonn, Koblenz and now Mainz. A brief stop every thirty or forty minutes.

Like a bloody commuter train, he thought.

The train began to move and gathered speed. He called for his bill and paid it, hoping that there wouldn't be a problem because he was using Dutch money in Germany. There wasn't. The only difficulty was that he wasn't sure how much the meal had cost or how much to tip—he didn't want the waiter to think him mean. Some of the coins were no larger than shirt buttons and looked very insignificant; he pocketed those and put three of the larger ones on the table, then hurried from the car in case he'd made a mistake.

The two women who had entered his compartment at Duisburg had evidently got off at Mainz. The man who had come aboard at Bonn was still there, however, along with a newcomer, a tall, hatchet-faced man in a tweed suit and black turtleneck. The two men either knew each other already or were getting acquainted—O'Rourke couldn't tell which, for

they were speaking in a foreign language. German, he supposed. Both of them struck him as shifty types, and he made
a point of ignoring them. Settling into his seat by the window
he reviewed the trip so far.

Apparently the days were even shorter in Holland during
the winter than they were in England—the sun hadn't come
up until the train had left Utrecht, more than an hour after
its departure from the Hook. And even when the sun had
come up, it hadn't been bright.

He opened a fresh packet of cigarettes and lit one. The
late sunrise was an advantage, but the density of population
along the railway line offset it. Cities, factories, farms—there
wasn't a mile that didn't have people living or working on
it. The kind of people who were early risers, too.

On the other hand, the roads in Holland seemed to be
excellent, and so did those in Germany. Furthermore, the
train itself was even better than he'd hoped it might be. He'd
walked through every coach. There was no second class. Each
coach had lavatories at both ends and automatic doors that
worked easily.

Sooner or later Cochran would have to use the lavatory.
The question was when. It was impossible to know in advance
whether or not he would feel the need to relieve himself before the train pulled into a station, and if so, which
one.

The compartments seated six people and offered no privacy.
The fact that he'd had this one to himself all the way to
Utrecht was pure chance. In any event, the partitions that
separated the compartments from the corridor were of glass,
as were the sliding doors.

He put out his cigarette and thought about Cochran. He
wished he knew how heavy he was, how young, how strong—
such things could make a difference. So could Cochran's habits. As it was, O'Rourke realized, he had no information at
all about the bugger, and there wouldn't be time to gather

any. He couldn't blame Garwood for that, of course. Garwood had probably phoned him as soon as he'd found out who had the money. Nevertheless, it made the planning more difficult.

The train slowed. O'Rourke had pocketed the timetable he'd found at his seat at the Hook of Holland, and now he consulted it. The explanations were in German, but he could follow the sequence of cities. He checked his watch. Mannheim.

The man who had come aboard in Bonn stood up and reached for his suitcase and his fur-lined coat. He said some words in the foreign language to the man with the hatchet face, bowed stiffly to O'Rourke and carried his coat and suitcase into the corridor.

The train stopped. O'Rourke watched the action on the platform. Evidently the weather was still cold. The people outside the train were emitting clouds of vapor from their noses and mouths.

The weather, too, was something that had to be kept in mind.

The train moved on. O'Rourke and the man with the hatchet face were alone.

"How far are you going?" the man asked.

O'Rourke was startled. He hadn't imagined that the man could speak English. You couldn't count on anything. "Geneva," he said. He really didn't want to get into conversation with anyone who looked so untrustworthy, but he didn't want to call attention to himself by being rude.

The man clucked sympathetically. "Such a long trip. Where did you commence?"

"At the Hook of Holland."

The man clucked again and shook his head. "Almost twelve hours you will be sitting."

"So?"

"You will be tired."

"My company doesn't like me to fly. Hard to replace, they say."

The man smiled. "What is it that you do?"

"Consultant. Scientific formulas."

"You are from the United States?"

O'Rourke blinked. It wasn't the first time he'd been mistaken for an American by foreigners. He was always surprised when it happened, however. He'd never been to the United States and he had no desire to go there, except maybe to Hollywood. The country as a whole was much too disorderly. Worse than Northern Ireland. "England," he said.

"Ah. And you are traveling on business for your company?"

O'Rourke nodded. Inquisitive bastard, he thought.

"I am the same. I am meeting with my employers in Baden-Baden. We are having a small conference. You have been to Baden-Baden?"

O'Rourke shook his head.

The man described it. A scenic place, a health spa, not many kilometers from Karlsruhe. At the beginning of the Black Forest. He was driving down from Karlsruhe. The road was very good.

O'Rourke grew interested. His mind began to work rapidly. Once more he consulted his timetable. Karlsruhe was the next stop. He put the timetable back in his pocket and said in a more friendly tone than he'd used before, "I'm always going to conferences here and there. I get quite tired sometimes." He placed his hand on the armrest, so that the man could see the bracelet. At the same time he noticed that the man was wearing a gold wristwatch that was very thin and had a strap of black crocodile skin. He might buy himself a similar watch, he thought, when he collected the three thousand. He would prefer a gold strap, though.

The man went on to explain, gratuitously, that he too traveled more than he cared to. He was a designer of store and office interiors. His home was in Frankfurt, but he'd been in Mainz overnight, and from Baden-Baden he was going to see a client in Zürich.

Designer, thought O'Rourke. Not as good as a consultant, but not bad either. "How long are you staying in Baden-Baden?"

"Five days. After the conference we will make a small holiday there."

"If the place is as nice as all that, I may fly up and have a look. I have some free time after my meetings. Is there an airport?"

"Yah."

"What hotel will you be at?"

"The Hotel Bellevue."

"And you're hiring a car, are you?"

"No, I am not hiring. Our representative from Hannover is meeting me at the train, and together we are driving."

"I see. Convenient, like." O'Rourke lit another cigarette. His thoughts were racing now. He looked out the window. The train was passing through the outskirts of a city. "Howard is my name," he said. "I may look you up in a day or so."

"It would be a pleasure." The man took a card case from his pocket and handed O'Rourke a card. Klaus Ranken was his name.

"My cards are in my suitcase, I'm afraid," O'Rourke said.

The train was losing speed perceptibly.

"Karlsruhe," said Ranken. He put on his coat and assembled his luggage.

O'Rourke gave him a broad smile. "It's been nice chatting."

They shook hands, and Ranken left the compartment.

The train came to a stop. O'Rourke put out his cigarette, lowered the window and leaned out. He saw Ranken being greeted by a man in a brown fur hat. The two of them started walking along the platform toward the stairs.

O'Rourke threw on his coat, grabbed his suitcase and got off the train.

12

Cochran folded the vest and put it back in the drawer. He was going to have to run the risk.

He moved restlessly about the flat as he adjusted to the idea. There was no denying that it *was* a risk. But the odds were overwhelmingly in his favor. Thousands of people did it every year—why shouldn't he, just this once? And anyway, even if it wasn't the best course, there was no satisfactory alternative.

Finally, his mind made up, he left the flat and went by Underground to Liverpool Street station.

The Sealink office wasn't crowded. The only people ahead of him were a young husband and wife who were purchasing second-class tickets for the Friday-night crossing. They soon completed the transaction, and he stepped up to the counter.

"I'd like to find out about checking a suitcase through from London to the Hook of Holland," he said.

"Aye," the clerk replied, "and what would ye be wanting to know?"

"How I go about it."

"All ye have to do is pay."

"What happens then?"

"Ye get receipts."

They went through the procedure in detail. It was slow work, for while the clerk was willing enough to dispense information, he dispensed it like a leaky faucet, one drop at a time. The cost of checking a suitcase to the Hook of Holland was one pound seventy-five. After paying, the passenger received two receipts. One he kept, the other he presented with the suitcase at the Port-a-bag counter. The attendant there put a "HOOK OF HOLLAND" sticker on the suitcase and attached the receipt to it. The passenger had nothing more to worry about. His suitcase would be waiting for him in the baggage-claim area at the terminal in Holland. All he had to do in order to retrieve it was hand over the duplicate receipt.

Cochran thanked the clerk and went to the Port-a-bag counter, where he confirmed what he'd been told. Then he took the Underground back to Knightsbridge.

He'd learned little that he hadn't expected to learn. He'd merely reassured himself that the Port-a-bag service was no more intricate than he'd imagined. He'd seen it used often enough and had been tempted to try it before. The only drawbacks were the one-in-a-thousand chance that the suitcase would be misdirected and the fact that the baggage-claim area at the Hook of Holland was under the surveillance of the customs inspectors. On one occasion he'd seen them question a passenger who was claiming a suitcase and make him open it for examination.

But in all other respects it was safe. And for this trip it was necessary.

Emerging from the Underground, he crossed Hans Crescent and walked into Harrods, where he spent an hour looking at luggage. He saw several pieces that would serve his purpose, but he postponed making a final decision.

As he was standing in line to get on the escalator, he heard a familiar voice call, "John!"

He swung around.

It was Kitty. And Ruth Watts was with her.

He stepped out of the line. The two women came up to him. Kitty gave his arm an affectionate squeeze. "What a coincidence," she said. "We were just talking about you."

He'd been thinking about the future. He struggled to pull his thoughts back to the present. "Oh?"

"It was nothing bad, I can assure you. Was it, Ruth?"

Ruth smiled and said, "Not at all."

"But it will be, if you don't offer to give us tea," Kitty added. "We're exhausted. Such crowds! You'd think this was the last Christmas that's ever to be."

He made another attempt to shift mental gears. "Tea? Is it teatime? Yes, I guess it is. Well, sure."

The three of them rode down to the lobby and went outside. Cochran began to collect himself. "Where would you like to go?"

"How about Maison Verlon?" Kitty suggested.

"O.K." Maison Verlon was a tiny patisserie a block away, on Pavilion Road. He and Kitty had often gone there during the months they were together, but although it was just around the corner from where he now lived, he'd never gone there since. Too many memories, he supposed.

There was only one unoccupied table, and they took it. Nothing had changed, Cochran thought as he looked around. The gray-haired lady who had tended the counter before was still tending it, the frail Thai girl was still waiting on tables, and the scent of freshly baked pastry was as inviting as ever.

The memories assaulted him.

"Don't you, John?" he heard Kitty say.

He came out of his reverie. "Don't I what?"

"Like the mince pies here."

"Yes, they're very good."

She frowned. "You seem abstracted. Is anything wrong?"

"No. Nothing." He made an effort to get with the conversation and by degrees succeeded. Kitty and Ruth had spent the past two hours in the china and glassware departments at Harrods, he gathered, and Ruth had been overwhelmed by the beauty of some of the pieces they'd seen.

"You like dishes?" he asked her presently, by way of joining in.

"They're not dishes, some of them," she replied. "They're works of art. It's like going through a museum."

She was different today, he thought. The self-consciousness had vanished. Even her appearance had improved. Her eyes were brighter, and her face was less pinched.

"Yes," said Kitty. "If the British could make cars and machinery as well as we make china, I daresay we'd have no economic problem at all."

The waitress glided over to the table. She gave Cochran a shy smile of recognition. Kitty again told Ruth that he liked the mince pies. Ruth said she would try one.

"So will I," Kitty said. "And tea."

"Make it three," said Cochran. "But with coffee—white."

"Tea," Ruth said.

The waitress glided away.

The conversation reverted to china. The expression on the women's faces was animated. Cochran concluded that in spite of the dense crowd in the store they'd had a thoroughly good time, and that the constraint of the preceding evening had been lost forever somewhere between the Minton and Royal Doulton displays. He recalled that Harriet too had admired fine china, but he quickly forced the recollection from his mind.

"If you like fancy plates," he told Ruth, "you ought to see the Wallace Collection."

Kitty gave him a look of surprise. "That's true! I hadn't thought of it! I'm sure Ruth would love to see the Wallace Collection. And not just the plates." She continued to eye him, no longer with surprise but with expectation.

He guessed at what she was expecting. "I sometimes go there," he said uncomfortably, "to look at the armor."

Kitty nodded eagerly.

He yielded. What the hell, he thought, it would only take an hour or two. And the Electors of Bavaria weren't all that unbearable. "If you're not doing anything in the morning," he said, "I'll be glad to show it to you."

Kitty turned to Ruth. "It's quite worth seeing. And I have an appointment with the dentist in the morning."

Ruth seemed embarrassed. "Really—I—"

"Gainsborough's 'Mrs. Robinson' is there," Kitty said. "The full-length one."

"Well, I—"

"Unless you have something else to do," Cochran said.

The color rose in Ruth's face. "It isn't that. It's just that I—well—"

"Splendid," Kitty said with finality. "You'll love it."

The waitress appeared with their orders, and after that the conversation faltered. Cochran had the feeling that he'd been manipulated, yet he knew that he hadn't been. He was the one who had mentioned the Wallace Collection. He drank his coffee and ate his mince pie in silence.

Presently Kitty glanced at her watch. "Oh, dear! I hadn't realized it was so late. Ian and I are going over to his sister's for dinner, and she simply loathes it when people are late. I really must dash." She got up. Cochran started to get up too, but she put her hand on his shoulder. "There's no need for you two to rush away because of me. Stay and enjoy yourselves." She gave Ruth a warm smile. "I'll ring you tomorrow afternoon and we'll plan something for Friday." Still smiling, she backed away from the table, and a moment later she was gone.

Ruth looked even more embarrassed than before. "You needn't, you know," she said at last. "Put yourself out on my account, I mean."

"Tell me something," he said. "How did you happen to hear of the Basil Street Hotel? It's not that well known in the States."

"A friend of mine recommended it."

"Cora Douglas?"

Ruth brightened. "You know her?"

"No, but Kitty's mentioned the name. Kitty probably suggested it to her."

"I believe she did."

"I'll be damned," he said, shaking his head. "Women baffle me. They always have. I guess that's why I have such a lousy track record."

"Did I say something wrong?" Ruth asked quickly.

"Not really. It's just that—" He shook his head again. "Well, so be it. I could use a drink. How about you? The pubs open at five thirty."

"Kitty thinks very highly of you," Ruth said uneasily.

"I don't doubt it. We were lovers for four months." He swallowed. "I'm sorry. I shouldn't have said that. Please try to forget it. Come on, I really do need a drink." He rose abruptly and signaled for the check.

The waitress brought it to him. He went to the cash register and paid. When he returned to the table, Ruth was still seated and staring at him.

"Come on, damn it!" he said sharply.

She stood up and put on her coat. He took her firmly by the arm and led her to the door.

"I should be getting back to the hotel," she said when they were outside. The hotel was less than fifty yards away.

He held on to her arm. "The hell you should."

She offered no further protest as he led her past the hotel, through the narrow passageway called Hooper's Court and out onto Brompton Road.

Inside the pub, he deposited her on one of the banquettes and said, "Is Scotch all right?"

She nodded.

He went to the bar, ordered two large Scotches and brought them back to the table. "I'm truly sorry for what I said," he said as he sat down. "I don't know what made me say it." He took a gulp of Scotch. "Kitty and Ian are the only real friends I have over here. I wouldn't hurt either of them for the world."

"Does Ian know about you and Kitty?"

He shook his head. "I've never asked Kitty, but I'm pretty sure he doesn't." He paused. "You must think I'm an awful bastard."

"No," she said, "but I think you're awfully angry."

He reached for his glass again, but after raising it halfway to his lips he put it down and pushed it away from him. "Angry?" He gave the matter some thought. "Angry. Well, yes, I suppose I am."

"Why?"

He gave that some thought too. "I don't like it when people feel sorry for me. Kitty feels sorry for me. I hadn't realized that before. It came as a shock."

"What's wrong with someone feeling sorry for you?"

"I don't like it. I don't like being felt sorry for. I am what I am, and whatever happens to me I deserve." He changed his mind about the Scotch. He picked up the glass and drank what was left in it.

"In other words, it's yourself you're angry at."

He gazed at the empty glass. "At myself? Yes, I guess that's one way of putting it. The fact is, I detest myself."

"I see. And what is there about you that makes you so detestable?"

He looked at her and perceived a genuine wish to understand. Then he looked away. She was little more than a stranger.

But presently the pressure became unendurable, and he said, "I killed the one person in the world I really loved. I killed my daughter."

13

He walked slowly back to his flat. It was after midnight. He could still feel the warmth of her lips on his. He felt dazed. And drastically changed. He was neither Steve Donner nor John Cochran; he was someone new.

The lights were on in the lounge, as they'd been when he'd left it a few minutes earlier to walk Ruth home. The cognac glasses were still on the table, hers full, his empty. The furniture was standing exactly where it had stood before. Yet somehow everything seemed different.

He went to the window. He could see the Basil Street Hotel. He wondered which room was Ruth's, and what she was thinking, and whether she was feeling as altered as he. She probably wasn't. The dam blocking her emotions hadn't cracked, as his had.

She'd been affected, though. Her eyes had registered that. So had her kiss.

He left the window and went to the table where the cognac

glasses were. He drank what was in Ruth's glass, then poured himself some more. The glasses had been a gift from Kitty.

He smiled. Ruth too had been a gift from Kitty.

"You'll get over it when you meet the right person," Kitty had said.

She couldn't have known that Ruth, whom she'd never met, would be the right person. She'd merely done what she could, and hoped. And succeeded.

He stretched out on the sofa and sipped the cognac. He supposed he should be ashamed of himself. In venting six years' accumulated anger and remorse he'd lost control to a degree he hadn't thought possible. Yet he didn't feel ashamed. He felt relieved of an intolerable burden.

The worst of his outburst had taken place in the flat. They'd only stayed at the pub for the one drink, then he'd taken Ruth to dinner at Mes Amis, the French restaurant across from Harrods. By the end of the meal he'd told her about his childhood—how his parents had separated when he was three, how both of them had remarried and had other children, how he'd been shunted back and forth, finally winding up with his maternal grandparents, who had raised him. He'd also told her about his marriage.

But back in the flat, where he'd brought her for an after-dinner drink, he told her about his divorce.

The marriage didn't seem a bad one to him. In fact, if anyone had asked him, he would have said that it was better than most. He'd known Harriet slightly for two years, but they didn't start going together until the last months of his senior year at college. She'd recently broken up with the assistant professor she'd been having an affair with and was at loose ends. Steve had been involved with a number of girls, often with two or three at a time, but with none seriously. Girls weren't his principal interest. He didn't have a principal interest. He was an adequate student, a member of the first-string track team, and popular; but he had no deep sense of commitment to anyone or anything. He seemed to get along quite well without it.

He began sleeping with Harriet almost immediately, and the week before graduation he proposed to her—if it could be called proposing. Actually, it was more in the nature of a suggestion. But, whatever it was, she said that she thought marriage would be nice, and on the first of that July, in a small ceremony at his grandparents' house, they became husband and wife.

The sense of commitment came later. After he'd been drafted. Somewhere near Da Nang. The morning he saw his best friend, John Cochran, blown to bloody pulp by a land mine. When it dawned on him that if he hadn't tripped and fallen behind, he might have been the one who stepped on the mine. He had no great metaphysical thoughts on the matter, but he did suddenly begin to feel that he had a destiny to live out and that some people and some things were more important than others.

Harriet was important. His work was important. And, even when Harriet was carrying her in the womb, Stephanie was important.

It was Harriet's idea that he should apply for a job with the Federal government. A cousin of hers had married a man who was with the Department of Health, Education and Welfare, and they had a nice house in Washington, D.C. Steve wasn't enthused. He had a chance to become a claims adjustor for an insurance company, and he wanted to take it. But at Harriet's urging he went to the Federal Job Information Center to find out what was available. He learned that the accounting courses he'd taken in college might enable him to become a Treasury Enforcement Agent and his status as a Veteran gave him an added advantage. He pictured himself as an investigator, and the picture appealed to him. Six weeks later he took the Civil Service examination and passed it. He became a Special Agent in the Customs Department at the GS-5 level.

That was the beginning of the good years.

It was a combination of factors that made them good. First there was his job. For reasons he didn't know and never tried to analyze, he was particularly expert at it. He got along well with the other agents, his superiors liked him, he made rapid progress. After a six months' training program at the Treasury Agents School in Washington, he was promoted to the GS-7 level. He felt successful.

Then there was his standard of living. Until Stephanie was born, Harriet worked, and with her salary added to his they were able to save enough to buy a house in a new subdivision. It was only a two-bedroom place, but it had a family room and a patio and was better than anything he'd lived in before. He was proud of it. Harriet was a shrewd manager. She respected money and handled it well.

But above all there was Stephanie. She was a beautiful child, and from the day she was born she was a source of astonishing happiness to him. As, apparently, he was to her. She seemed fascinated by him when she was still in her cradle, following him with her eyes and responding to him more readily than to her mother. And as soon as she could crawl, she began trailing him around the house with such obvious delight that Harriet sometimes became annoyed.

"You spoil her," she said.

"No, I don't. But why don't we even things out—have another child, one that *you* can spoil?"

"We can't afford it."

"Sure we can."

But the second child was not to be his. It was to be Hugh Jordan's.

The jolt was totally unexpected. And shattering.

He'd spent the better part of two months on a case involving the theft of two truckloads of Scotch, then had gone to work immediately on a case involving a gang that was smuggling into the United States large quantities of hand-painted dolls made of compressed hashish. The whiskey investigation had necessitated repeated trips to Michigan, and the hashish case had taken him to southwestern Texas. He'd been home occasionally for periods of a few days, but for most of the spring and early summer he'd been away.

He'd returned after participating in the arrests of the hashish smugglers to be greeted by the news that Harriet had fallen in love with another man and wanted a divorce.

At first he refused even to consider divorce. There were rough spots in every marriage. They'd work it out. He didn't know, of course, that Harriet was pregnant and that the child she was carrying wasn't his. But when she finally told him, adding that it was too late for an abortion even if she'd wanted one, which she didn't, he continued to stand his ground. It didn't matter that the child wasn't his; he could learn to love another man's child.

In the end, Harriet simply moved out. He came home from work one evening to find a note on the living-room table: "I'm sorry it has to be like this, but there's no future for either of us. My lawyer is Daniel Barnes. Call him—947–5322. H." Harriet was gone, and so was Stephanie. He located them at Hugh Jordan's. Harriet wouldn't come back.

At that point he was willing to concede that the marriage was finished. But what he wasn't willing to concede was that Stephanie should be taken away from him.

The lawyers pointed out to him that he was in no position to raise her himself, that she would still be his daughter no matter whom she lived with, that Jordan was a wealthy man who could give her advantages. And it wasn't as if Steve would never see her again; he'd have visitation rights.

The lawyers eventually convinced him. Harriet waived alimony and was awarded custody of Stephanie. Steve could have her every week from noon on Saturday until six o'clock unday evening and for two weeks each summer.

In January Harriet gave birth to a son, Hugh Wesley Jordan,
r.

And in March the Jordans sold their house and moved to
'lorida. If Steve wanted to see his daughter, he had to go
here to do so.

He filed a petition, but there was nothing in the divorce
lecree that prevented Harriet from living in another state.
His suit was dismissed. Even if it hadn't been, if the case
1ad been decided in his favor, the court order would have
1ad to be enforced in Florida, which presented problems.

He made two trips to Florida to see Stephanie. She was
obviously not thriving. Both times she sobbed pitifully when
1e left.

Then he made a third trip to Florida.

He called for Stephanie on a Sunday morning, promising
to bring her home in time for dinner. But by dinnertime
they were in Boston, boarding a plane for England as John
Cochran and his daughter, Eunice.

"But how did you manage?" Ruth asked. "I mean the passports and everything."

"You can't be a Treasury agent for any length of time
without learning where and how to get false passports," he
explained. "And it wasn't any spur-of-the-moment decision,
don't forget. I'd been thinking about it and planning it for
months. I'd sold everything. I took the money I'd just inherited
from Gramps. I—well, I knew what I was doing. There were
no slip-ups. I'd thought everything through. The trouble is,
I didn't think it through far enough." His voice broke.

Ruth said nothing.

It took him a while to get himself under control. "I knew
it wouldn't be easy for me to get a job in England. We make
it tough for foreigners to work in the States, and other countries do the same thing. Besides, I had a new identity. I

couldn't come up with references or anything. I thought had enough money to see us through. I thought eventuall I'd find something. It turned out that I didn't.

"For the first week we lived in a hotel," he went on afte a pause, "but I didn't feel safe there. I didn't know wha Harriet and Jordan were doing about trying to find us, bu I knew we'd be found more easily in a hotel, so I got us flat. It was a furnished place in Chelsea—it wasn't much just three rooms over a store, and the price was unbelievabl high, but it was better than living in a hotel—and the landla dy's sister was a widow, and she was willing to baby-sit witl Stephanie while I was out looking for work. It seemed lik a good move. But it—it really wasn't."

It was several minutes before he could continue.

"Monday," he said. "It was a Monday. I remember that I'll never forget. A Monday. Stephanie seemed to have caugh a cold. That's what I thought it was. A cold. That's what told Mrs. Westbury. The sitter, that is. I mean, she saic her neck hurt her and her head hurt her. Stephanie, I mean It was December, you see, and the flat wasn't as warm a we were used to, especially Stephanie coming from Florida so it was possible, you know. A cold, I mean. Mrs. Westbury felt her forehead. We didn't have a thermometer, you see We hadn't needed one. She had a slight temperature, she said. I felt her forehead too. She *did* have a temperature Not much, though, it didn't feel like. Mrs. Westbury saic she'd keep her in the apartment. They'd play, and she'd give her a light lunch. I remember that. A light lunch, she said. It didn't seem serious. And I thought I had a lead on a job. I went out. But the lead didn't amount to anything. I was disappointed. I went to a pub. I stayed there until two thirty, when it closed. Then I walked around. I was beginning to realize how hard it is for a foreigner to get work over here. Well, I didn't get home until half past four. Mrs. Westbury was beside herself. Her sister was there too. They were arguing

bout whether to take Stephanie to a hospital. They didn't
now whether I'd approve. I still can't believe it. A simple
hing like that. Taking a sick child to a hospital. She was
lying, for God's sake! She'd broken out in a purple rash over
lmost her entire body and she was burning up with fever,
he was delirious, and there they were arguing about whether
'd approve of taking her to a hospital.

"Well, I grabbed her and wrapped her in all the blankets
ve had and ran downstairs to get a taxi. I didn't even bother
o ask them where a hospital was. Just a hospital, I thought.
Any hospital. And there I was on King's Road, where you
:an always get a taxi, and all of a sudden I couldn't get one.
It was raining, and Stephanie was getting wet, and there I
vas standing at the curb, and no taxis. It seemed like forever
before I got one. I told the driver to take me to a hospital.
He wanted to know which one. I said I didn't know which
one. Any hospital, I said. The nearest one. He couldn't take
me to a hospital, he said, if he didn't know which one. I
began to yell at him. Finally, I guess, I got through to him.
There were hospitals all around the place, only I didn't know
it, and anyway maybe it wouldn't have made any difference
by then. But at any rate he took us to St. Luke's, and an
hour after we got there Stephanie died. She'd had meningitis."
His voice suddenly rose. "So what I did is, I stole Stephanie
from her mother and brought her to a strange country and
let her die of meningitis!"

He got up and refilled the cognac glass.

The tempest had come and gone. He felt more at peace
than he had at any time in the past four years. There was
now one human being besides himself who knew his story.
He'd told Kitty about Harriet, but he'd never mentioned
Stephanie. As far as Kitty was concerned, he and Harriet
had had no children.

The only thing he hadn't told Ruth was the nature of

the work he did for Arlen. When she'd asked him what kin
of job he'd finally found, he'd merely replied, "The kind
shouldn't be doing," and she hadn't pressed him for detail
Instead, they'd gone on to talk about other aspects of th
kidnaping. Ruth had said she couldn't believe that Harrie
hadn't made some attempt to trace him.

"I suppose she did," he'd agreed. "I've thought about i
and thought about it. But I'd been pretty careful. I had
friend . . ." He hadn't gone on. The less she knew abou
that, the better. A former Treasury agent who had left th
agency and become successful in business. His company plane
The wild drive from Coral Gables to the airport in Palm
Beach. The harrowing flight through the rain to Boston. There
was no need to compromise Doug at this point—or Ruth
either, for that matter. He'd merely said, "And it's possible
that she didn't try too hard. She never really *loved* Stephanie
and she had another child—perhaps by now she has two or
three kids. I don't know. All I know is that nobody's caught
up with me. But I can't go back. Even if I weren't prosecuted
for taking Stephanie, I'd be in trouble—it's a Federal offense
to leave the country on a false passport."

"But you can never feel entirely safe, John." She'd continued to call him John, not Steve.

"I know. All I can do is hope."

She'd looked at him. "You don't mind if I hope with you,
do you?"

He'd taken her hand. "Two hopes are better than one."
And shortly after that he'd walked her home.

The two men descended the steps to the underpass, turned right, crossed the concourse of the terminal and went outside to the car-park.

O'Rourke followed at a safe distance.

The car was a gray Audi.

The man in the fur hat unlocked the boot, and Ranken tried to fit his luggage in, but apparently the boot was already full, for he ended by putting the larger of his cases on the back seat.

O'Rourke stepped between two other parked cars and watched the Audi being backed from its stall. As it turned, he noted the license number and model. What he saw pleased him. He had a considerable knowledge of cars, and this one, he felt, would serve admirably.

He looked across the road. Not much of a town, he thought. A provincial nowhere. Cold as a witch's tit, besides.

He saw a sign—"SCHLOSS-HOTEL"—and studied the build-

ing to which it was attached. The building didn't impress
him favorably, but he decided that the Schloss-Hotel was prob
ably as good as Karlsruhe had to offer and at least it wa
convenient—directly opposite the station. He walked over to
it.

The receptionist said something in German.

"I'm English," O'Rourke informed him irritably.

"Good afternoon," said the man.

Mollified, O'Rourke said that he wanted a room. "One
of your better rooms," he added.

The room he was given wasn't as good as he would have
liked, but it was adequate, and from the window he got a
different perspective on the city from the one he'd had at
ground level. What he'd taken to be the countryside was
actually a large park. The railway station, instead of being
at the center of the city, was at the edge. Karlsruhe was more
than a hamlet; it was a place of some consequence, with a
population, he estimated, of several hundred thousand; but
most of it lay beyond the park.

He stood at the window for some time, orienting himself,
then sat down on the bed, lit a cigarette and considered his
needs.

Half an hour later, he went downstairs, left his key at the
desk and returned to the railway station. On his way across
the concourse, he'd noticed a bank and a variety of shops.
He went into the bank, converted a hundred pounds into
Deutschmarks and made a tour of the shops. Among them
he found a bookstall. He began to browse. Presently he saw
what he wanted and made his purchase: three maps—one
of Karlsruhe, one of Germany and one of Western Europe—
and a German-English dictionary.

Tucking the bag under his arm, he crossed the concourse
to the booking office. There he ran into difficulty: none of
the booking clerks spoke English. He tried one window after
another. At each the man misunderstood him and tried to

ell him a ticket. He was exasperated and on the verge of osing his temper when one of the passengers who was standing n queue at an adjacent window intervened. The station for Baden-Baden was called Baden-Oos, she explained in English, and many trains went there from Karlsruhe. She directed O'Rourke to the timetables that were posted on the wall around the corner, but then, as if fearful that that wasn't enough, she gave up her place and escorted him. The white timetable listed arrivals, she pointed out; the yellow one, departures. O'Rourke noted that there was a train to Baden-Oos almost every hour.

He gave the woman a smile and a nod and left the station. It wasn't going to be easy, he decided, in a country where those who ought to know English didn't. It was, in fact, going to be bloody difficult. A chap had no one to rely on but himself. But then, he'd more or less expected that. For all their goose-stepping, the Nazis had lost the war, hadn't they? In everything but making cars and binoculars, they were thick-headed.

He walked past the entrance to the hotel and turned right, following the mental chart he'd made while standing at the window of his room. When he came to the broad thoroughfare that bordered the park, he turned left. A street sign told him that he was in Ettlingerstrasse. He opened his map of the city. He was able to determine from the map where he was, but there was nothing on it to indicate which was the main shopping street. For that, he would have to rely on instinct, and his instinct told him that if he walked far enough in the direction he was going he'd come to it.

He closed the map, quickened his pace and cleared his head of old thoughts. The situation called for an open mind.

He walked for several blocks, then stopped abruptly when he heard something that sounded like the trumpeting of an elephant. It seemed to be quite near.

He looked around. He was the only pedestrian on the pavement, but the motor traffic was heavy. Ridiculous, he thought. There were no elephants in Germany.

He walked on.

The sound was repeated. He was positive it was that of an elephant, and became alarmed. He didn't like elephants. He didn't like wild animals of any sort. Seeing the entrance to an office building, he started toward it.

A lion roared.

He stopped in his tracks. Elephants. Lions. He glanced toward where the sounds had come from. He heaved a sigh of relief. The stupid Germans had put their zoo right next to one of the city's busiest streets.

Returning to the street, he continued in the direction he'd been going. Idiots, he thought. Suppose one of the animals escaped. Germany was even worse than Spain.

The park seemed to go on without end. He began to question his own judgment. It was possible that he wasn't heading toward the shopping section, after all. But he recalled the view from his window—this *had* to be the right way. It was just that the distance was greater than he'd imagined.

He came to a major crossroads. He checked the signs and consulted his map. Ettlinger Tor-Platz. The plan of the city resembled a wheel; dozens of streets radiated like spokes from a central hub. The map showed he was approaching that hub. He nodded to himself and crossed the road.

Five minutes later he reached his goal. It was called Kaiserstrasse and was the Piccadilly of Karlsruhe. Gratified, he turned left and joined the horde of rush-hour shoppers.

In an English city he would have known exactly where to find what he wanted. But this wasn't an English city; this was bloody Germany, and anything could be anywhere. So he walked slowly and studied the displays in the shopwindows with great care.

The shop that seemed most promising was called Hammer & Helbling. The window display featured cooking utensils, power tools, wall paint and outdoor furniture. He made note of the location of the shop, then walked on. Presently he saw a comforting Woolworth sign. Germany wasn't so different, at that.

He went into Woolworth's and began systematically to study the merchandise. The store was very crowded, and it was difficult to get near some of the counters, but he took his time and let himself be jostled. The counter that held his attention longest was the one on which Christmas gift-wrapping supplies were arranged. He examined the items on it thoughtfully, but didn't see anything suitable. Nor did he see it at the automobile-accessories counter. He continued his search. And among the electrical accessories, next to an assortment of extension cords and light switches, he spotted what he was looking for.

The tape came in all the primary colors, he noted with satisfaction. He took one spool from the counter and peeled off a small strip. The outer surface was plasticized and shiny, and the adhesive quality was good. But the width was less than that of his index finger, and there appeared to be none that was wider. It would do, but it would take a long time to apply. He decided to seek elsewhere.

Slipping the spool into his coat pocket, he left without paying for it and went back to Hammer & Helbling.

A quick tour of the ground floor revealed little besides crockery, glassware and kitchen equipment. He climbed the stairs to the floor above. Tools and building supplies of all sorts filled the large sales area. He went up one aisle and down another. No tape. Finally he approached a sales clerk.

"You speak English?" he asked.

The young man shook his head.

O'Rourke swore under his breath. "Does anybody?"

The clerk gave him a blank look.

O'Rourke took the tape from his pocket and pointed to it. "This," he said.

The clerk's expression brightened. He led O'Rourke to the other side of the room and stepped behind a counter. O'Rourke nodded briskly, for on a shelf behind the counter was exactly what he wanted. He flexed the fingers of both hands toward himself. The clerk transferred some of the tape from the shelf to the counter. O'Rourke repeated the gesture. The clerk transferred some more.

O'Rourke examined a spool of the black, measured the width against his fingers and decided that it would serve the purpose nicely. After visualizing several color combinations, he made his selection. Six spools of black tape that was as wide as his three middle fingers together and twelve spools of red that was slightly wider than his thumb. More than he would need, he was certain; but better too much than too little.

He handed the clerk a wad of banknotes and let him take the proper amount. Then, package in hand, he went downstairs and out to the street.

Resourceful, he thought. That's what a chap has to be.

He wasn't finished, however.

Standing at the curb, humming cheerfully, he viewed the building across the street. An array of flags proclaimed it to be Hertie Markt, which meant nothing to him. But the building was large, and there was a heavy flow of traffic in and out. It could be a department store, he decided, and worth investigating.

A department store was what it was, but the aisles were so crowded that he was inclined not to proceed. Evidently it was true what they said about the Germans having most of the money in the Common Market. But, he told himself, since this was the case, the other department stores would be just as busy, so he might as well stay in this one.

There was nothing on the ground floor that remotely resembled what he was after. He rode the escalator to the floor above. Nothing there either. He went on to the next floor, and his eyes lit up.

Thirty minutes later he left the store with a long carton containing a disassembled luggage rack for the roof of an automobile and a small bag of the tools necessary to assemble and attach it.

His shopping expedition was complete. In an hour and a half he'd acquired everything he needed. And without knowing a word of the language.

He smiled to himself. Kenneth O'Rourke was Kenneth O'Rourke, even in Germany. Still, he thought, recalling his experience at the station, not knowing the language could cause trouble.

At this point his luck ran out. He was unable to find a taxi. Putting down his other packages, he consulted the dictionary he'd bought. "Taxi" was *taxi*, and "stand" was, among other things, *standplatz*. He stopped several passers-by and put the two words together. The Germans understood his question, but he couldn't understand their answers.

He ended by having to carry maps, luggage rack, tape, tools and reading material, with a combined weight of over seven kilos, two miles across the city to his hotel.

He spent the evening in bed, studying the maps.

15

The room was totally dark when he awoke. He reached for the switch and turned on the bedside lamp. His watch showed four thirty.

He'd been dreaming about Trumper. He couldn't recall the activities in which Trumper had been engaged or what his own role had been, but the dream had been disturbing, and now he felt vaguely uneasy.

This was unusual. He wasn't by nature a worrier. Worry, in his opinion, was a waste of time. Either a chap could depend on himself or he couldn't. If he could, there was nothing to worry about; if he couldn't, worry didn't help.

But while O'Rourke was certain that he fell into the dependable category, he was equally certain that Trumper didn't. For all his many appealing qualities, Trumper was essentially a clod. He didn't think things through and was inclined to take whatever path was easiest. That was why he kept getting into trouble.

Making a back-rest of the pillows, O'Rourke lit a cigarette and considered the past twenty hours. He felt more confident now than he had when he'd started. But Trumper . . .

He threw back the covers, got out of bed and reached into the pocket of his suitcase. He'd torn the half-page advertisement from the American medical magazine at the last minute and brought it with him. He found it, took it back to bed with him and reread it. But he already knew the properties of the drug, and the rereading did nothing to lessen his anxiety. It wasn't Thiopental that bothered him; it was Trumper.

Bringing the advertisement with him had been a mistake, he realized. He should have given it to Trumper. At the time, he'd considered that he was being emphatic enough. But he really hadn't been. When dealing with someone whose head was screwed on as lightly as Trumper's, you had to show him in black and white exactly what you wanted.

He picked up the telephone.

"Bitte?" a man inquired presently.

"I'd like to place a trunk call to London, England," O'Rourke said, as carefully as if he were speaking to Trumper. "Operator-assisted, if you don't mind." He gave Trumper's number, pausing after each digit, then asked, "Do I make myself clear?" and repeated it.

The man said he would ring when the call was completed.

O'Rourke put out his cigarette and immediately lit another. He drummed his fingers on the bedside table as he waited.

After some minutes, the telephone rang.

A sleepy Trumper muttered something unintelligible.

"Greetings, love," O'Rourke said.

"Whozis?" Trumper asked thickly.

"Kenny. Who does it sound like?"

"Kenny?" Trumper seemed to come instantly awake. "Are you back already?"

"Of course I'm not back already," O'Rourke said with annoyance. "I just got here."

"You did? Where are you?"

"Germany, stupid. What have you done about what I told you to get?"

"It's taken care of. It'll be here on Saturday."

"How did you take care of it, Trump? How can you be sure?"

"I spoke to Herbert."

"Bentham?"

"Yes."

O'Rourke felt relieved. Herbert Bentham was an airline steward on the London–New York service. His connections in the States were exceptionally good. He could, for a modest fee, get almost anything, even on short notice. "When does he leave?"

"Tomorrow. Or today, I guess it is. What time is it?"

"Five o'clock in the morning here. Thursday. Now, when does he leave?"

"Today, it must be. He lays over one night, I think. At any rate, he said he'd bring it on Saturday. That's all right, isn't it?"

"That's all right, but I want you to call him as soon as I finish speaking to you. I want you to be sure you ordered the right product. Do you have a pencil and paper?"

"I have a pen. Will that do?"

O'Rourke sighed. "Yes, that'll do," he said patiently.

"I'll have to get it." Trumper put down the telephone.

O'Rourke drummed his fingers until Trumper was again on the line.

"I've found it," Trumper said, sounding pleased.

"Clever of you," O'Rourke said dryly. "Now write this down, exactly as I tell you." He spelled out the name of the drug, making Trumper repeat each letter as he gave it to him. Then a new thought entered his head. "How much did I say I needed?" he asked.

"You said a hundred milligrams."

"I want to change that. I need *two* hundred milligrams. Write that down too. Two hundred. Got it?"

"Two hundred," Trumper echoed.

"Good. Now I want you to call Bentham immediately I hang up and give him the exact spelling and tell him I want two hundred milligrams instead of one hundred."

"He won't appreciate being woken up like I am, in the middle of the night, Ken."

"I don't care whether he likes it or not. Do it. Understand? Because if anything goes wrong I'm going to break both your bloody arms, and you can count on that."

"I'll do it, Kenny. You don't have to lose your temper."

"I'm not losing my temper. I'm merely explaining the situation."

"Yes, Ken."

O'Rourke's tone softened. "I miss you, Trump. We'll spend Sunday together. Maybe we'll get Gillian again. Would you like that?"

Trumper said he rather would.

O'Rourke smiled and hung up. Then he put out his cigarette and turned off the light. However, he'd already had more sleep than he was accustomed to and he couldn't doze off again, so after tossing and turning for a quarter of an hour, he got up and began to study the dictionary.

The first word in the German-English section was *aal:* "eel." The last was *zyste:* "cyst." Bloody ridiculous, he thought, and skipped to the English-German section. There were four German words for the plain English article "a," he found, and three for something as uncomplicated as "lunch." It was no wonder that the Germans couldn't understand foreigners— they probably couldn't even understand each other. Finally

he decided that the dictionary was useless—it was impossibl
to learn a whole stupid vocabulary in a few hours—and h
threw it into the wastepaper basket.

Closing his eyes, he let his thoughts drift over the move
he'd made since leaving his flat. He was satisfied that they
were the proper ones. The difficult part of the job still lay
ahead, but the call to Trumper proved that he was considering
every possible misstep, that he was operating at peak efficiency
and that as a result nothing would go wrong.

At a quarter past seven he got up, shaved and took a long hot bath. Then he dressed and inspected himself in the mirror. Dark blue suit, white shirt, tie with regimental stripes—the over-all effect was excellent, he thought. Like the managing director of a multinational corporation, a man who because of his exceptional abilities had already reached the top of the ladder at the age of twenty-nine. A pair of glasses would add to the image, he conceded, but he didn't own one, and anyway Ranken had first seen him as he was now.

Over breakfast he again devoted himself to the maps of Germany and Western Europe. The route was fixed in his mind, but he wanted to review the distances and estimate the length of time the trip would take. Between five and six hours, he decided at last, knowing that in such matters he was never wrong.

After a second cup of coffee, he spent a few minutes studying the map of Karlsruhe, noting the location of the small blue squares with white P's that indicated parking facilities.

Finally he packed. The clothes he'd worn the day before went into the suitcase, and around them he fitted the maps, the spools of tape and all the tools except the screwdriver. That he put in the inside pocket of his jacket.

The desk clerk who'd been on duty the preceding afternoon was back at his post.

O'Rourke deposited his room key on the counter and said, "I plan to go to Baden-Baden this afternoon. What hotel do you recommend? I'd naturally prefer one of the better ones."

The clerk mentioned some names. The Hotel Bellevue was among them.

O'Rourke considered. There was the question of showing his passport when he registered. "Not the Bellevue," he said. "One of the others. What was the first one you said?"

"The Brenner's Park. Very expensive, most elegant."

"I think I'd prefer that one. Will you make the reservation for me? I'll pay for the call."

The clerk hesitated. O'Rourke put a ten-mark note on the counter. The clerk looked at it. "That is not necessary. The charge will appear on your bill."

O'Rourke shrugged and pocketed the money. The clerk asked him for how many nights he wished the room.

"Three," he replied. It was the first number that came into his head.

Five minutes later a room had been reserved, and O'Rourke went out to the street. He didn't relish the prospect of the long walk along the park and past the zoo, but he felt that it was necessary for him to acquaint himself with the traffic pattern.

The parking facilities were numerous. Most of them were situated between Ettlinger Tor-Platz and the hub of the wheel, which, according to the map, had a large U-shaped building in the very center of it. The building was labeled "Schloss." Having found the first few car-parks exposed, attended and not at all to his liking, O'Rourke crossed Kaiserstrasse and walked toward the Schlossplatz.

The Schloss was a bloody castle!

Broad paths flanked by statues and trees led across the vast forecourt to the main entrance. Drawn by curiosity, O'Rourke started along one of the paths, but a sign caught his eye and he stopped. The sign said, "TIEFGARAGE KASSE U. W.C." A flight of stairs beside the sign led to an underground foyer. He recalled the map. There *had* been a car-park at this point. He smiled. Of course. The entire area in front of the castle, statues and all, was nothing more than the landscaped roof of a subterranean garage.

He descended the staircase and looked around, his smile broadening. There was a cashier but no other attendant. He posted himself against one wall and waited for someone to come along. His wait was short. Two young men appeared at the foot of the steps. One of them presented a ticket to the cashier, gave her some money and received what appeared to be a metal token. He and his companion then walked through a doorway.

O'Rourke followed them.

The garage was the cleanest and best organized he'd ever seen. Walls divided it into sections that were neither too large nor too small. Each aisle was marked with a letter, each stall with a number. The fluorescent lighting was bright enough but not too bright.

From a distance he watched the two men get into their car, then walked back to the up-ramp he'd seen and waited for them to pass. Within a minute they did. The driver deposited the token in a slot, and the automatic gate swung up.

Ideal, thought O'Rourke.

He returned to the foyer.

"Are you open twenty-four hours?" he asked the cashier.

The look she gave him indicated that she hadn't the slightest idea what he was talking about.

He drew a large circle with his finger and punctuated it with dots to denote hours.

She seemed to comprehend. She nodded and said, *"Vierundzwanzig."*

He had to be certain, though. He pointed to a pad of paper beside the cash register and made writing motions. She handed him the pad and, when he indicated he had nothing to write with, a ballpoint pen. He wrote, "24?"

She nodded again.

"Thanks, love," he said, and went up the stairs, humming. *"Kasse"* had something to do with "cashier," *"vierundzwanzig"* was "twenty-four" and the self-parking garages in Germany were quite like those in England. He felt considerably edified.

He walked along the Schlossplatz until he came to a down-ramp and made a note of the street that gave access to it. Then he consulted his watch. It was just ten o'clock. He had hours to kill. Deciding against visiting the castle, he returned to Kaiserstrasse and gave himself up to recreation.

He spent an hour window-shopping men's haberdashery, imagining how he'd look in various items that attracted his attention. He'd look very well in most of them, he thought, although some were definitely for less sporting individuals.

After a while, he began to explore the side streets, and on one of them he found a sex shop. He went in.

It was inferior to the sex shops in London, he found. The general atmosphere was most provincial. Nevertheless it offered enough to keep him interested for the better part of an hour, and there was a dildoe that he was tempted to buy as a souvenir for Trumper. But after giving the matter due consideration, he left the shop without making the purchase. The dildoe was no better than the ones Trumper had.

At twelve thirty he came to a restaurant that made a favorable impression on him, and had lunch.

At two o'clock he returned to the hotel, paid his bill and collected his suitcase and the box from Hertie Markt. An hour later he was on a train bound for Baden-Oos.

17

Was it too early to call her? Cochran wondered. She might still be asleep.

But then again, she might not. And it would be nice to have breakfast together.

Perhaps she wouldn't want to have breakfast together, however. Perhaps she'd had second thoughts about him. Perhaps . . .

He got out of bed, looked up the number in the telephone directory and dialed.

"Basil Street Hotel."

"Ruth Watts, please."

The operator rang. Ruth answered.

"Good morning," he said. "This is the nut who lost his head last night. I hope I didn't wake you."

"No, you didn't," she said. "I was just getting ready to go down to breakfast."

"Well, don't. I want to apologize for making a fool of

myself, and I apologize best over the breakfast table. Wait for me."

And before she could reply he hung up.

He showered, shaved and dressed in fifteen minutes, feeling reckless, foolish, excited, and utterly adolescent.

Still damp under the chin and between the shoulderblades, he burst into the hotel and took the steps two at a time.

She was waiting for him by the hall porter's desk.

He glanced at her face and knew instantly that everything was all right.

London was transformed. The buildings dazzled him. The fountains and monuments were magnificent. The traffic was stimulating. He'd never seen so many interesting-looking people in any one place.

He'd been to the Wallace Collection on several occasions. He'd liked it. But he'd never been deeply thrilled by it. And now he was. Because Ruth was.

The Sèvres, Limoges and sixteenth-century Venetian tableware delighted her, as he'd thought they would. So did the silk brocade wall coverings, the crystal chandeliers and the delicately ornamented French furniture. To his surprise, however, she also showed interest in the early Turkish, Persian and East Indian weapons that he particularly liked. And when they came to the superb fifteenth- and sixteenth-century German armor she gazed at it with fascination. He hadn't forgotten that the German armor was there; it just hadn't occurred to him that it would have a special significance for her. But of course it did. It was the first time she'd ever seen anything that had actually belonged to the families she'd been reading about for years, and she was awed. Minutes went by before she could speak, and then she was capable of only a single comment: "It was more than adaptability, wasn't it? It was also cruelty."

He saved the most impressive room for last. The long gallery that extended across the entire width of the first floor and contained the best-known works in the collection. Titian, Rembrandt, Velásquez, Gainsborough—Ruth moved without speaking from one painting to another, and he followed, watching the changing expressions on her face, trying to guess at her thoughts and to share them. She seemed to be especially touched by Rembrandt's portrait of his son, "Titus," and Gainsborough's "Mrs. Robinson." But she spent the most time in front of Reynolds's "Nelly O'Brien"; she returned to it twice.

Her words when they left the building and were standing in Manchester Square, looking back at it, had nothing to do with any individual painting, however. She said, "It's all so very different."

"Different?"

"From the United States, I mean." She paused, as if to clarify to herself exactly what she did mean. "It was a *house.*"

"Well, sure."

"One family lived there."

"The Duke of Manchester, originally, if I've got it straight. Then the Marquess of Hertford. Then his illegitimate son, Sir Richard Wallace."

"But one family—one man, really—*owned* all that."

He smiled. "A guy needs a roof over his head and a few wall decorations."

"No one in the United States was ever that rich. In relation to everyone else, I mean."

"Sure they were. Richer. Vanderbilts, Astors, Morgans—"

"No. Things were spread around more. We never believed in primogeniture."

"Come again?"

"When the oldest son inherits virtually everything. Fortunes were kept intact for hundreds of years. Even when there was no legitimate heir, everything went to one person, like this Richard Wallace. The history of Europe would have been entirely different if it weren't for that. There would have been far less bloodshed."

"Well, now," Cochran said admiringly, "I've found me a deep one." Unexpectedly, a dark thought crossed his mind. The thought of Evans. "It's not like that anymore. Inheritance taxes have changed the whole scene." He shoved the thought of Evans from his mind. "Come on, I'll show you around the neighborhood."

She took his arm. He walked her over to Baker Street and showed her the home of William Pitt. Then they went back across Manchester Square to the house on Bentinck Street where Gibbon had lived and the one on Wimpole Street from which Elizabeth Barrett had eloped with Robert Browning. Ruth stood in front of the Barrett house for several minutes in silence. He could see that she was moved.

"She loved late," she said finally, "but she loved well."

He said nothing, but as they walked toward Oxford Street, the words echoed in his ears. Was it possible to love late but well?

They entered New Bond Street, and he pointed out other landmarks.

"How come you know all these places?" Ruth asked.

"I've walked every street in London," he replied. It was hardly an exaggeration. "That's what I did after Stephanie died. Come on—you must be hungry. I'll buy you lunch."

The pub was one he'd never been to. They ordered shepherd's pie and beer. Ruth ate with relish. She'd never heard of shepherd's pie, she said.

"The English don't appreciate it," he told her. "They take it for granted."

She returned to the subject of primogeniture. Her theory, she explained, was that it was a by-product of monarchy. In the ruling family the oldest son inherits the crown, and the practice filters down. Eventually stagnation sets in, though, and stagnation is the cause of revolutions.

She admitted that the German armor she'd seen had made her wonder whether she was going to like Germany. There had been a certain fierceness about it that shocked her. She began to talk about the Teutonic temperament.

"You're doing it again," Cochran said. "Like the other night."

"Doing what?"

"Using history to avoid talking about yourself."

"Am I?" She colored slightly. "Yes, I suppose I am. I don't mean to."

"Yes, you do."

She hid for a moment behind her beer mug. Then she put it down. "Not consciously, John. It's just that I—well, I haven't had a very high opinion of myself lately. Divorce can do that. But you know that better than I."

He nodded.

"It's not like it was with you, though. I had no illusions that it was a good marriage. Not after the first few months. He was unfaithful from then on. I simply put up with it. For twelve years I put up with it. Don't ask me why—I don't know. There were no children. He didn't want children, and I couldn't have them, and at first it worried me. I felt imperfect in a way, but then I began to think that maybe it was just as well—we weren't the sort of couple that should have children. He was never home, and I worked, and I was around children all day, and what can I tell you? But what happened was that after a while my ego began to come apart. I had to leave him in order to save myself. I'm not sure that I have, though. Saved myself, that is."

"You did the right thing," Cochran said fervently.

"Did I? I don't know. I thought it was the right thing. But being alone isn't good either. I've found that out these past few months. It's been no better for me than being half married was."

"Is that why you came over here?"

"Partly, I guess. But it's not the main reason. The main reason is that I've had it with high-school students. For a long while they were enough. Good ones, bad ones—I've taught them all, and I've been fond of them. But I want to go on to the university level, and I need a doctor's degree for that." Suddenly she clenched her hands and brought them down on the table. "There has to be more to life than what I've known, John! There just has to be!"

He covered her hands with his. "There is."

She looked first at his hands, then at his face. She gave him an embarrassed smile. "Now wouldn't you rather hear about the Electors of Bavaria?"

"No," he said firmly.

18

Darkness had fallen by the time they came out of the National Gallery. The rush-hour traffic around Trafalgar Square was heavy. It was impossible to get a taxi. They walked over to the Strand and joined the queue at a bus stop.

They were almost at Piccadilly before Ruth asked where they were going.

"Back to my place," Cochran told her. He'd been thinking about it for an hour. But all of a sudden he felt peculiarly inexperienced.

She offered no objection. But he noticed that she clasped her hands more tightly around her pocketbook.

Neither of them spoke during the ride.

They got off at the Knightsbridge stop, and he guided her across the frantic intersection. When they passed the Basil Street Hotel, he pretended it wasn't there.

He turned on the lights in the lounge and took Ruth's coat. He hadn't thought when he'd brought her there the night before how the flat might appear to her, but now he did. It was only half furnished and not at all orderly. He'd taken it at Kitty's urging, in order to be near where she lived, although he'd known that the rent was higher than he could afford. It was going to take him a long time to put together enough money to buy the necessary furniture.

"One of these days I'll get around to finishing it," he said apologetically. "I need a chair over there, and a table there, and—" He went on to list some of the other purchases he intended to make, realizing as he was doing it that he was talking simply to hide his nervousness.

"Good heavens!" Ruth exclaimed. "I just remembered. Kitty said she'd call me this afternoon. She must think I'm lost. Where's the telephone?"

"In the bedroom." He wished that he'd taken time to make the bed.

Ruth hurried from the room.

He got the bottle of Scotch from the kitchen and poured himself a large drink. As he sipped it, he could hear Ruth's voice. Strange, he thought. This was the first time in over four years that someone other than himself was using his telephone. Four *years*. He shook his head. Incredible.

Ruth's voice rose. "Glorious. I wouldn't have believed that there could be so many absolute masterpieces in a single building."

She was talking about the National Gallery, he knew. She'd been flabbergasted by it.

He stopped sipping and took a large swallow, then carried the glass into the bedroom.

Ruth was sitting on the unmade bed. He dropped down beside her. She smiled at him. He slid the telephone from her hand and said into it, "Hi there."

"John?" Kitty said.

"John," he affirmed. "You said something about you and Ruth doing something together tomorrow afternoon. Would it be all right if she didn't? There are some places I'd like to show her."

Ruth shook her head in protest, but he nodded emphatically.

"But I don't understand," Kitty began, then stopped. "Or do I?"

"Well," he said.

"Of course it's all right," Kitty said. "Friday is my afternoon for the hairdresser's anyway. But—"

"I knew you'd understand. And as for the rest of her stay, since it's going to be so short—"

"John!"

"Well," he said again.

"I'm amazed."

"Do you remember what you said? Well, you were right."

"I said so many things. I mean—"

"I'll remind you, one of these days. But to save Ruth any embarrassment, I think I'd just better hang up and hope you really do understand." And before she could reply, he put the telephone back on its cradle.

"You shouldn't have," Ruth said reproachfully.

He finished the Scotch. "The hell I shouldn't." He put the glass on the table, beside the telephone.

She sighed. The reproachful expression vanished. "What did Kitty say?" she asked. "You said you'd remind her of it."

He grinned. "She said I'm gun-shy but that someday I'd get over it." He put his arm around her.

She didn't resist, but she turned her head away.

He put his other arm around her and forced her to look at him.

"I'm afraid," she said. "It's been so long. I'm afraid I'll be a disappointment."

He stroked the side of her face. "It's been a long time for me too. I'm afraid of the same thing." He drew her closer and eased her backward. "But I want you, Ruth. I want you more than anyone I've ever known."

He awakened once. He didn't know what time it was, or care. But he was awake for what seemed a long while. Ruth's arm was across his chest, and her face was touching his shoulder. He could feel her breath on his arm. She was breathing lightly, evenly.

He stared at the ceiling, intensely aware of the woman beside him. And of the fact that the impossible had happened—that he'd fallen completely in love.

He couldn't imagine living the rest of his life without her.

Yet he knew that somehow he was going to have to find the strength to do just that.

O'Rourke finished filling out the registration form and looked around him.

Distinguished, he thought.

An attendant from the reception desk accompanied him to the lift. As they passed the bar and lounge O'Rourke glanced quickly through the doorway. Like a château, he concluded.

"Is this satisfactory?" the attendant asked after showing him the room.

"Not bad," O'Rourke replied.

The attendant left, and O'Rourke bounced on the bed. It was very comfortable. Then he opened the door to the balcony. The air was cold, but he remained outside for several minutes, surveying the scene. His balcony overlooked a park. Beyond the park were steep hills dotted with villas. Most of the trees and shrubs in the park were bare, but the effect was nevertheless attractive, and people were walking on the footpaths. A narrow river, terraced into a series of neat little ills, rushed briskly along beside the park.

Agreeable, he thought. Probably frequented by bankers and he like. And he had a vision of himself in a purple silk dressing own, breakfasting on the balcony in the sunshine.

But there was no sunshine now. The sky was gray and henacing. He hoped it wasn't about to snow.

A porter brought his luggage.

O'Rourke closed the door to the balcony, went into the athroom and examined his appearance. It satisfied him.

He returned to the ground floor. He kept the room key n his pocket.

The doorman was helping a middle-aged couple from a Mercedes. The woman had a Pekingese tucked under her rm. O'Rourke waited until the doorman had finished his hore, then approached him.

"You speak English?" he asked.

"Yes, sir."

"Where's the Hotel Bellevue?"

The doorman gave him directions. The Bellevue was less han a ten-minute walk. It was the first hotel beyond the wimming bath on the Bertholdstrasse, beyond the large garden pavilion. It was best reached by the walking path along he Lichtentaler Allee.

"What's that?"

"The park. You go to the first street, Bertholdstrasse, and urn right. Across the bridge is the Lichtentaler Allee. There ou turn left. It is very short."

O'Rourke tipped him and set out.

Swimming pool, tennis courts, formal gardens, a large hotel. A sign on the footbridge across the river said that the hotel vas the Bellevue. The doorman had been right. Seven minutes.

O'Rourke crossed the footbridge, opened the gate and proceeded across the hotel grounds to the car-park.

The Audi was parked near the gate. It was locked. The car-park was unattended.

Humming, O'Rourke entered the hotel. A quick tour of the ground floor left him with the feeling that he was back in England, in a first-class hotel in a second-class city. Dark paneled walls, heavy furniture upholstered in cut velvet, oil paintings of people who had undoubtedly belonged to the nobility, and an abundance of potted plants. Such places depressed him. He stopped humming.

"Mr. Klaus Ranken?" he said to the hall porter.

The hall porter rang the room. There was no answer. O'Rourke chose a chair near the door and sat down to wait.

He waited for forty-five minutes.

At twenty minutes to six three men came into the reception hall from outdoors. One of them was Ranken.

O'Rourke hastily got up and approached him. "You remember me?" he said. "Howard, from the train. I said I might come up here after my meetings. Well, so I have."

Ranken regarded him for a moment with a blank expression. Then he brightened. "Yah, the train. Geneva." It was clear that he'd been drinking. His face was flushed, his eyes were glassy. And his companions were in the same condition. O'Rourke recognized one of them as the man who had met Ranken at the station in Karlsruhe.

"My principals flew me up in their plane," O'Rourke explained. "Lovely little trip. How is the congress progressing?"

"The congress? Ah, the congress. It is many meetings. But men must have pleasure also. They must forget business. Permit me to introduce my associates. Herr Schmidt, Herr Ganzhorn—Herr—I regret—your name again?"

"Howard. James Howard."

"James How-vard."

O'Rourke shook hands with the two men. He made a mental note of the fact that the one with the Audi was Ganzhorn. "May I give you gentlemen a drink?" he offered.

Schmidt shook his head. Ranken appeared undecided.

Ganzhorn said, "A small glass of wine is possible. A most small glass of wine."

Schmidt announced that he was going to his room. Ranken said that if Ganzhorn was going to have a glass of wine he would too. Schmidt left, and O'Rourke accompanied the other two into the bar.

During the next twenty minutes he learned that twelve members of the firm were in Baden-Baden, but not all of them were staying at the Bellevue. One was staying with relatives, two were at the Atlantic, and the other six were at the Europäischer Hof, where the meetings were being held but where, because of another congress, it had been impossible to reserve enough rooms for the entire group. They had had a meeting before lunch and another after lunch. Then they had adjourned to the bar. Some of them were getting together after dinner, however, to try their luck at the Casino.

"Casino?" said O'Rourke.

Baden-Baden was famous for its casino, he was told. He didn't know that, he said—he wouldn't mind trying his luck also. Whereupon he was invited to join the party.

He agreed to meet Ranken and his contingent in the reception hall of the Bellevue at nine o'clock.

At ten minutes past six he left them, went back to the Brenner's Park and asked the doorman for directions to the Casino.

A quarter of an hour later he was there. And was almost incapacitated by the opulence of the place. It exceeded anything he'd ever fantasized and fulfilled fantasies he hadn't yet progressed to. The thick red and green carpets, glittering chandeliers, gilt statues, expanses of mirror, marble and rich-looking wood filled him with such awe that he was distracted from his purpose. What should have taken him less than an hour took him nearly an hour and a half, and in order to

accomplish it in even that length of time he had to kee
reminding himself that he wasn't a tourist and three thousan
pounds were at stake.

He explored the gambling rooms first, out of sheer curiosity
In order to do so, he had to buy an admission ticket, whic
involved showing his passport and filling out a form. He hes
tated over this, but persuaded himself that he wouldn't b
the only British subject to have bought a ticket that day an
in any event his form would simply go into a pile with th
others.

From the gambling rooms he went on to investigate th
bars, the restaurant, the cloakroom facilities and the men'
lavatory. He climbed the broad stairway to the first floor
but found nothing useful there—only a concert hall—and
quickly returned to the ground floor.

The final stage of his inspection took him to the under
ground level, where he spent twenty minutes. A wide corrido
linked the stairway from the ground floor with a garage. Along
the corridor were showcases with some of the priciest merchan
dise he'd ever seen—mink coats, gold watches and cosmetic
that only the very wealthy ever used. Gazing at it, he had
the feeling that he was being underpaid; a clean sweep of
the showcases would bring in more in a few minutes thar
he was earning from a ten-day enterprise. But he knew nothing
about the German system of criminal justice, he decided
and he had no wish to learn.

Bypassing the entrance to the discothèque, he proceeded
to the garage. It was almost a duplicate of the one in Karlsruhe
Located under the park in front of the Casino, it was ap
proached by a down-ramp with an automatic gate. Each aisle
was numbered and had its own door leading into the lower
level of the Casino. Unlike the garage in Karlsruhe, however,
the cashiering was done by a machine, and he wasn't sure
of the method. He had to wait for some minutes in order
to see someone go through the procedure. The man put his

parking ticket in a slot. Numbers appeared in lights, telling how much to deposit. He put the coins into something that resembled a telephone box, and a large token dropped into a tray. The token, O'Rourke deduced, was what opened the exit gate. After the man left, he examined the equipment until he was certain he understood it, then went up to the ground floor, changed a ten-mark note into small coins at the bar and, with some reluctance, left the building.

The following hour he spent walking back and forth between the Casino and the Brenner's Park, for the shops were closed and he didn't know where to get a map.

The distance was less than half a mile, he estimated, but there was no street that served both buildings. There was, instead, a complicated arrangement of one-way streets that led into other one-way streets. What under different conditions should have been no more than a two-minute trip would take at least five minutes.

After observing the traffic flow for some time, he came to the conclusion that the indirect route was actually the best, and began to walk it. The Lichtentaler Allee, along one side of which most of the hotels were located, was a lengthy park but a narrow one. By using the street that bordered the opposite side of the park, he would circle the Brenner's Park and approach it from the other direction.

This final walk took him around a large theater and along the lower slope of the closest of the hills he'd seen from the balcony of his room, on a road called Friedrichstrasse. Narrow and poorly lit, it rose and fell and curved as it followed the contours of the slope. He could see little other than the trees of the Lichtentaler Allee on his left and the indistinct shapes of villas hidden by shrubbery on his right. The night air was very cold.

But he felt rewarded when he came to the end of Friedrichstrasse and found himself at Bertholdstrasse, less than fifty yards from the hotel.

Although he was thoroughly chilled, he didn't go inside. He continued on to the Bellevue, arriving at exactly nine o'clock. The Audi was still parked where it had been before. He hurried into the reception hall to warm himself.

And at ten minutes past nine Ranken and Ganzhorn appeared.

20

Schmidt would not be accompanying them, Ranken said—
he was feeling unwell from drink. But they themselves were
eager to begin the sporting.

O'Rourke had anticipated that there might be a problem
concerning the use of the car, for he'd observed that, despite
the cold, many people in Baden-Baden seemed to enjoy walking. He'd marshaled a number of arguments in favor of driving,
including the possibility of snow. He was even prepared to
come up with a treacherous knee injury, if necessary. But
the problem didn't arise, for the two Germans explained, apologizing for the delay involved, that they'd agreed to pick up
the co-worker who was staying with relatives.

When they came to the car, O'Rourke noticed that Ganzhorn took the keys from the right-hand pocket of his loden
coat.

Ranken got into the front seat, O'Rourke into the back.
The engine sounded as if it was in good condition. The

car seemed to handle well. The imitation fur covers o the two front seats called attention to themselves—an ad vantage.

They traveled for almost a mile in the opposite directio from the Casino, entered the driveway of a house, and Ranke got out of the car. But before he reached the front door, opened and a stocky little man emerged. He got into th back seat of the car with O'Rourke, and they were introduced The man's name was Werben.

Ranken and Ganzhorn were sober now, but Werben ha either had less to eat or more to drink, for he gave off distinct odor of wine and chattered in his native language laughing boisterously at his own remarks, all the way to th Casino.

The machine at the gate dispensed a parking ticket, an Ganzhorn took it. He held it in his hand while he sought parking stall. He found one in Aisle C, and the four me got out of the car.

O'Rourke had expected the parking ticket to go into th right-hand pocket of the loden coat along with the car keys and it did.

And from that moment on, everything went exactly accord ing to his number-two plan.

They proceeded along the corridor and up the stairs in group. They took off their coats at the same time and put them on the long counter of the cloakroom. The charge wa fifty pfennigs per person, payable in advance. With a smil and an "Allow me, gentlemen," O'Rourke whipped out the correct change and gave it to the attendant before the othe three could even get their hands into their pockets. He took all four receipts and distributed them, keeping Ganzhorn's and giving Ganzhorn his. The four of them proceeded to the counter to fill out their forms for admission tickets.

O'Rourke went through the motions of discovering that he'd left his passport in his overcoat and told the others to go on to the tables, he'd catch up with them. Then he returned to the cloakroom and claimed Ganzhorn's coat.

He carried it some distance toward the stairway, took the keys and parking ticket, returned the coat to the cloakroom, where he explained to the attendant that he'd mixed up the tickets. As he'd expected, she hadn't the slightest idea what he was talking about and simply, for another fifty pfennigs, issued him another receipt.

He caught up with Ganzhorn at the entrance to the gambling rooms.

"Stupid of me," he said, "I gave you the ticket for my coat by mistake."

They exchanged tickets.

O'Rourke made another trip to the cloakroom and claimed his own coat. Putting it on a chair, he used the admission ticket he'd bought earlier to enter the gambling rooms.

He joined Ranken at one of the roulette tables and wished him luck. Then he spotted Ganzhorn and Werben at another table and spoke to them.

"Everything's O.K. now," he assured Ganzhorn.

The German smiled and nodded abstractedly. He was already following the spinning of the wheel.

O'Rourke resisted the temptation to place a few wagers. He left the gambling rooms, picked up his coat, paid into the vending machine the amount it demanded for the parking, and went immediately into the garage.

He regretted that he hadn't been able to use his number-one plan, which had been to pick Ganzhorn's pocket while he was absorbed in the play. This would have been easy for O'Rourke and would, in addition, have given him an opportunity to gamble for a few minutes himself. But, he conceded, he'd saved himself time.

He found the car and took the screwdriver from his pocket. He removed the license plates. Then he stepped over to the next car, a Ford Fiesta, and removed the plates from it, replacing them with those from the Audi. The Ford's plates he put on Ganzhorn's car.

Humming, he unlocked the Audi, backed it from its stall, drove to the exit, deposited the token and, when the gate opened, sped up the ramp to the street.

Following the route he'd chosen, he reached the Brenner's Park in five minutes.

He left the car with the engine running and went to the cashier's desk. "I have to leave sooner than I thought," he said, and gave his name and room number. "Please prepare my bill."

He rode the lift to the third floor, collected his luggage and rode the lift down again.

He paid his bill in cash, carried his luggage to the car and drove off.

Forty-five minutes later he was in Karlsruhe. It had been easier than he'd expected.

21

As he passed under the railway viaduct and emerged into Ettlingerstrasse, he had a moment of doubt. Was the garage the best place, after all?

He decided that it was. The light was better there than it would be on the street, especially on an obscure street; there was no danger of nosy residents or passers-by, no possibility of patrolling police cars; and it was too bloody cold to do the job outdoors.

But no matter where he worked, he would have to work fast.

His doubt dispelled, he headed toward Ettlinger Tor-Platz with the assurance of one who had lived in the city all his life and knew every crossing. He was doing what he was best at.

He found the entrance to the Schlossplatz Tiefgarage with no difficulty, took the ticket offered by the dispensing machine and drove slowly toward the farthest aisle. He'd expected the garage to be relatively deserted at that hour, and it was. Whereas almost every stall had been occupied during the morning, what he saw now were rows of empty spaces, with only an occasional car here and there.

The space he selected faced the garage's back wall. In the entire aisle there were only six other cars, but when he got out of the Audi he examined the license plates of two of them. The first letters of both were KA. For Karlsruhe, he deduced. He opted for the Volkswagen, and the Audi got a new set of plates for the second time. The colors were the same on all the automobile licenses in Western Europe, and hopefully the owner of the Volkswagen wouldn't notice the switch for several days. But it hardly mattered now whether he did or not.

O'Rourke lit a cigarette and set about his next tasks. First he removed the conspicuous fur covers from the front seats and threw them into the boot. Then he opened his suitcase and took out the plasticized tape.

Starting at the front of the car on the right side, just below the top line of the fender, he applied the narrow red tape along the fender to the door. There he cut it neatly, ran another strip across the door, cut it, ran a third strip from the door to the back of the car. He stepped away from the car to light another cigarette and check his work. The line of the tape had to be perfectly straight and appear to be continuous. It was and it did.

He proceeded to do the same thing on the left side, then applied the wide black tape in an identical manner, directly below the red. Satisfied that the black fitted snugly against the red, he went to work with another spool of red, attaching it below the black.

Finally he devoted himself to the lower portion of the car, running three bands in the same red-black-red combination between the front and rear fenders on each side and cutting each strip so that the doors would open without difficulty.

He strode six paces away from the car, did a swift about-face and looked at it as if he were seeing it for the first time.

With two parallel sets of racing stripes, it was transformed.

Humming, he unpacked the luggage rack and took his wrench from the suitcase. Then he lit another cigarette and began to attach the rack's crosspieces.

Presently he heard footsteps. He turned around. A woman was coming toward him.

He frowned. The nearest car was five stalls from where he was working. She passed it and continued in his direction. The best thing, he decided, was to ignore her. He dipped his ashes and went on with tightening a bolt. The footsteps grew louder, however. Evidently the woman was on her way to one of the cars on the other side of him.

But, to his surprise, instead of passing him, she strode over to him and began to speak angrily in German.

He stopped what he was doing and looked her up and down. She was a woman of about forty, broad-shouldered, wide in the hips, with a square jaw and a decidedly unpleasant expression. She bore a startling resemblance to Miss Althorp, who had accused him of cheating on his spelling paper and had sent him home with a note to his mother. He'd denied that he'd been cheating, and his father had believed him, but his mother hadn't. A proper beating she'd given him, too. Not for cheating on the spelling paper, but for not admitting the truth about it. A dishonest little wretch, she'd called him. And that was one of the times he had not been cheating.

A deep anger came over him. His face gave no hint of it, though. "I don't speak the language, love," he said amiably.

But either she didn't understand him or she intended to break the language barrier by sheer volume. Her voice rose. She shook her finger at him, another of Miss Althorp's habits. His anger deepened. He wondered how long the woman had been watching. Was it possible she'd seen him switch the license plates and had been spying on him ever since? He began to feel a coldness deep within himself.

Her voice rose even higher, and she shook her finger at him a second time. Then she pointed to the floor. He glanced down. The various parts of the luggage rack were scattered on the pavement, among the cigarette ends. So was the screw-driver. She *had* been spying.

"Bugger off," he said furiously, "before I lose my temper."

She got red in the face. Even if she hadn't understood the words, she'd understood the tone of voice—and didn't like it. She went right on, repeating words she'd used before, words that meant nothing to him: *"Rauchen verboten."* But now she added a new one: *"Polizei."* And *"Polizei"* did mean something to him. She was threatening to call the police.

"Oh, will you?" he said. And with that he took her by the arm, turned her around and gave her a push.

She uttered a cry of rage.

He began hastily throwing the pieces of the luggage rack into the car.

She uttered another cry. He looked up and saw her running heavily along in the direction of the cashier's office. He dropped his cigarette, grabbed the wrench and caught up with her. Once more he seized her by the shoulder, and this time he pulled her around to face him.

"Shut your filthy mouth!" he told her.

Her eyes widened with fear. She screamed. He slammed the wrench down across the top of her head. She sank to the floor.

He dragged her back to where the Audi was parked and knelt beside her. Her eyes stared up at him. There were trickles of blood from a wound under her hair and from her nose. He could feel no pulse.

Stupid old sow, he thought, and lifted her into the boot of the car. Her head lolled to the left. He tucked it into a orner of the boot and folded her legs, then tried to close he boot. It wouldn't close.

He rearranged the body. The boot did close.

His heart was pounding. He looked around. There was no one in sight. He waited. No one appeared. He took a deep breath, removed the parts he'd thrown into the car and went back to work.

Fifteen minutes later he walked to the foyer, paid for his parking, received his token and returned to the car.

As he slid behind the wheel, he noticed a sign on the wall that he hadn't noticed before. It said, "RAUCHEN VERBOTEN." Like the words the woman had used, he thought. He wondered what they meant.

He recalled signs in English car-parks. Some were directional signs with arrows that pointed to exits and ramps, others were warnings, such as "SLOW" and "NO SMOKING."

This sign had no arrow beside it.

He turned the key in the ignition. The engine started immediately. He eased the car out of the stall. Again he noticed the sign. Could *"Rauchen Verboten"* mean "No Smoking"?

He'd had a cigarette between his lips. She'd pointed to the floor. Was it possible that she'd been pointing not to the screwdriver but to the cigarette ends?

He guided the car to the end of the aisle and turned it in the direction of the exit ramp.

That was it. She'd been trying to tell him to stop smoking and threatening to call the police if he didn't.

Officious, he thought. Well, she wouldn't be sticking her nose into other people's business or telling them what to do, not ever again.

He gave an affirmative grunt. Worse luck for her than for him.

He deposited the token in the slot. The gate opened. He pressed down on the accelerator.

It was a quarter to one when he reached the highway. He waited until the light was green, then turned onto the access road. And within seconds he was speeding northward on E-4 toward Heidelberg and Mannheim.

The beam of his headlights caught a sign that said, "RAST PLATZ" and beside it were other signs with "P" and "WC" on them. He slowed and saw picnic tables and rubbish bins. The surrounding area was thickly wooded.

The road between Baden-Baden and Karlsruhe had been bordered by woods also. Evidently he could count on patches of dense shrubbery and evergreen trees for some distance along this road.

He made a quick decision. Pulling into the rest area, he turned the car so that the boot was facing the woods, then unlocked it and began to strip the body.

As he'd guessed, it was hard work, for in the sub-freezing temperature rigor mortis was advancing rapidly. He had to use the screwdriver to rip the dress and underclothes so that he could peel them from the twisted figure. But at last the job was done and he could drive on. A rest area was no place to dispose of a body, and he hadn't yet made up his mind what to do with the clothes.

But fifteen kilometers farther north he stopped again, pulled over to the shoulder of the road and, taking the body from the boot, carried it some twenty meters into the woods. He deposited it under a shrub. It would be discovered, but, if he was lucky, not for several days. And there would be no clothes to aid in the identification.

Finally, at a rest area north of Heidelberg he made his final stop. The clothes went into the carton that had held the luggage rack. The carton went into one of the rubbish bins. Forty-five kilometers separated the clothes from the body.

The woman's pearl earrings he kept, however. They would make a nice Christmas gift for Gillian.

Dawn was breaking when he pulled the car into the car-park beside the terminal at the Hook of Holland. It was twenty-five minutes past eight. The formalities at the Dutch border had been less troublesome than he'd feared.

The night ferry from Harwich had unloaded. There were a few vacant spaces in the car-park. He chose what seemed the most inconspicuous of them and brought the car to a stop facing the wire-mesh fence. The car was considerably dirtier than it had been when he'd driven it from the Casino in Baden-Baden, and with the racing stripes, luggage rack and new license plates it had the appearance of an altogether different vehicle. Even the interior seemed changed, without the seat covers.

He carried his suitcase onto the railway platform just as the boat train to Amsterdam was pulling out. He was tired and very hungry.

He went into the buffet and had a large Dutch breakfast of cold meats, cheese and bread. While eating, he pondered. What he wanted was a proper English-speaking travel agent, but he supposed that that was too much to expect; and his subsequent inquiries proved the supposition to have been correct.

There was, however, a booking clerk. And the booking clerk could comprehend his meaning.

O'Rourke went into the men's lavatory and soaked one of his shirts in a sink, then took it out to the car and cleaned the boot of the few bloodstains he could find. He also wiped the interior and exterior to remove fingerprints, just in case.

And when the day ferry sailed for England, at eleven fifteen, he was aboard. Sound asleep in one of the cabins on A Deck.

In one of the de-luxe cabins.

22

"No eggs," Ruth reported from the doorway. "No bacon either. All I could find were a loaf of bread, some cheese and a funny-looking pastry."

"That's a pork pie," Cochran said. "I was planning on having it for lunch yesterday." He propped himself up on one elbow. "But then you came into my life."

"Sorry about that."

He beckoned to her. She was wearing his bathrobe, and it almost touched the floor. She looked like a child playing grown-up. "Come here."

She walked over to the bed and sat down beside him. He put his arm around her. She ran her hand through his hair. "I couldn't find the toaster."

"That's because I don't have one. I use the oven." He pulled her toward him.

She put her feet up on the bed and nestled against him. "Was everything all right. I mean, really?"

"Everything was fine. Just fine. You know that."

"I'm glad."

They lay side by side, and for a while neither spoke. Finally Cochran said, "Do you *have* to leave on Sunday? Couldn't you postpone it?"

She didn't answer immediately, and he was beginning to think she wasn't going to, when she said, "I could postpone it. I don't think I should, though."

He regretted the weakness that had made him ask the question.

"I *must* go to Germany, John. It's my one chance."

"I understand."

They were silent again.

"You could come there, though," she said presently. "I'll have the apartment. You could visit me. And maybe later on I could come back here for a few days."

The partings would become increasingly difficult, he knew. And eventually she'd return to the United States, where he couldn't follow. He said nothing.

"Couldn't you?"

"Perhaps." A clean break would be best. Until Sunday they would be together. But after Sunday . . .

As if she sensed his thoughts, she drew away from him and sat up. "I'd better make us some toast and coffee."

She went into the kitchen.

He fought the mood that was beginning to settle over him. They still had forty-eight hours, he reminded himself as he went into the bathroom to shave.

He was drying his face when the telephone rang. Kitty, he supposed. He went into the bedroom and answered.

"Cochran?"

The voice gave him a severe jolt. It was Arlen's.

"Yes," he said.

"You have something important to tell me?" Arlen sounded more reptilian than usual.

Cochran's mind slowed. "Are you in London?" he asked, trying to keep it from stalling altogether.

"No. What's your message?"

Tell him? Cochran wondered.

"Breakfast's ready!" Ruth called from the kitchen.

Don't tell him?

"The girl said it's important," Arlen reminded him impatiently.

Cochran temporized. "I'm going away for a few days. Next week." He waited for Arlen to ask where he was going, to force the issue.

Arlen didn't. "So?"

"I'm going to be out of touch. I thought you ought to know."

"You just made a trip. I won't need you for a while. You should know that. Why did you go to the office? You know I don't want you to go to the office. You were stupid."

"I thought I ought to tell you. I thought—"

"The fact is, you didn't think."

"I'll be gone until the end of next week."

"You were very stupid. You know the importance of security. You should have better judgment than to try to contact me when I'm away. Don't ever do it again." He hung up abruptly.

Cochran put the telephone down. He'd burned the only bridge. And he had the feeling he'd made a mistake.

He turned around and saw Ruth standing in the doorway, smiling.

"The coffee's getting cold," she said.

They went into the kitchen. She'd taken the trouble to find the napkins and fold them into triangles and to make the butter into curls. He wondered as he sat down how much she'd overheard.

"Is anything wrong?" she asked.

He shook his head.

She sat down too. "I didn't mean to eavesdrop, but I couldn't help hearing you say you'd be away for a few days. Does that mean you're coming to Holland? Does it mean—?"

"No," he said sharply. He was immediately sorry for the sharpness. "No," he repeated, more mildly, "it means I have to go away for a few days on business."

"Where to?"

"Switzerland."

"But then—"

"No, Ruth, it does *not* mean I can come to Holland. Or to Germany either. It means—" He gave up. "Oh, hell, it means I'm trapped!"

She looked at him, but said nothing. She poured coffee into his cup.

"Don't look at me like that. I'm a prisoner in this goddamn country. Don't ask any more questions."

She offered him the plate of toast.

"I'm the prisoner of a man who's made me into something I shouldn't be."

"Have some butter."

Cochran reflected. "No, that's not true. I made myself into something I shouldn't be. He just employs me."

"The butter?"

He handed her the dish. "I love you, Ruth. So help me God, I do. But once you leave England . . . Oh, let's talk about something else. Tell me about the Electors of Bavaria."

Ruth poured coffee into her cup and buttered a piece of toast. "I've been thinking," she said. "The problem might not be as big as you think it is. Perhaps you should make an effort to find out."

"Find out what?"

"Where you really stand. The lawyer who got me my divorce, he specializes in such things. I mean he knows private investigators, he has contacts. He could have someone talk to your wife, find out what's going on with her. It could be done in such a way—I mean, they use women agents and men who know how to go about things like that—she'd never even know she was being questioned. Maybe she's willing to forget the whole thing. You yourself said she has another child, and possibly more by now. Maybe you're making an exile of yourself when it isn't necessary."

"She wouldn't be willing to forget." He drank some coffee. "But even if she were, there's the business with the passport."

"Once you got back to the States, you could destroy it. No one need know you ever used it."

He smiled. "You'd make a good crook, honey."

"I'm merely trying to be realistic. You've been so involved in it all, you've lost your perspective. All I'd have to do is call Todd—he's a very good lawyer, he'd know how to handle it."

Cochran shook his head. "It wouldn't work, Ruth. Stephanie was her daughter as well as mine. And I was a Federal agent, for Christ's sake." But he felt a faint stirring of hope. So faint that it was barely above the threshold of perception. "I love you, though. I can't yet believe you actually exist."

Ruth refused to be diverted. "I wish you'd consider it, John. You have nothing to lose."

"O.K., I'll consider it. Where would you like to go today? Westminster Abbey is what I had in mind. And after that— well, there's the Houses of Parliament and Downing Street, and then we could come back here." Time was so short. So terribly short.

"Whatever you say. More coffee?"

He nodded. "There's only one thing I have to do first," he said, "and I can do it while you're getting dressed. I have to run over to Harrods for a few minutes. I have to buy a suitcase."

23

"Where are you?" Trumper asked. Once again he sounded sleepy and confused.

"Home, love. Home," said O'Rourke. "Where'd you think I was—on the bloody Equator?"

"How am I supposed to know? Last time, you were in Germany." Trumper sounded irritated too.

"I *said* I'd see you today. Any problems?"

"Problems?"

"With Bentham."

"Oh. No. He didn't like being woken up in the middle of the night, any more than I do. I told him what you said and that it was important. He was going to ring up New York, he promised. The stuff would be ready by last night. What time is it?"

"Just past eight. Time you was up."

"Why? It's Saturday, isn't it?"

"You don't want to lay about all day. It's not good for you. What time you coming over?"

"After I see Herbert. That's what you want, isn't it?"

"Yes, old cock. That's what I want."

"Along about three, I expect."

"I'll be waiting." O'Rourke hung up, then dialed Gillian's number.

Gillian didn't answer.

Annoyed, he went into the kitchen and made himself some breakfast. The breakfast and a long hot bath with aromatic bath salts restored him to good humor.

After shaving, he put in some time at the bedroom mirror. He appeared to be none the worse for the trip. Possibly he'd lost a pound or two, but, however much it was, he would soon regain it. And he'd scratched his right hand. He'd noticed that in the car. Dragging the German woman through the shrubbery was how he'd done it, he supposed. He hadn't been aware of the scratch at the time, and it wasn't serious—it was already beginning to heal—but it reminded him of the woman's stupidity. People insisted on meddling. They never seemed to learn.

But his suit was another matter. The trousers were mud-stained, and there was a tear in one of the legs. This too had probably happened when he was dragging the woman into the shrubbery, and was something to be concerned about. The suit had cost him a hundred and sixty quid and had looked better on him than anything else he owned. The mud-stains could be removed and the tear could be mended, but the suit would never be the same.

He put his soiled clothes in the hamper and discarded the shirt he'd used to wipe the car. Another twelve quid he was out of pocket. He hadn't expected to bring back much of the three hundred Garwood had given him for expenses, but he hadn't expected the trip to cost him any of his own money either. And when you considered the suit and shirt, it had.

Garwood was going to have to reimburse him.

He spent twenty minutes putting the flat in order, and nother five reviewing the advertisement for Thiopental, then ettled down with some back issues of *Dominators* and *Bound nd Beaten*. He could never decide which of the two publications he preferred. Both had lovely pictures.

There was no doubt that Bentham's mission had been a uccess. Trumper's face was flushed with pride.

"Just what the doctor ordered," he said, handing the package to O'Rourke with a flourish. "That'll be fifty quid, if ou don't mind."

"I don't mind," said O'Rourke, mentally adding the fifty o the bill he intended to present to Garwood. He opened he package and examined the contents. Two vials in their original paper boxes. Provided, no doubt, by an employee of one of the New York hospitals. Amazing country, the United States. Corruption everywhere. The hospital employee had even included a syringe, which O'Rourke hadn't requested and didn't need. "Very nice."

Trumper beamed. "Don't we have that sort of thing over here?" he asked.

"Without a doubt. But I expect the name would be different, and this is the name I heard of. You know me, Trump— I don't take chances. Substituting is taking a chance. Besides, it's harder to get things from a British hospital."

"Is it?"

"I think so. Give me your coat, love. I'll make you a drink."

"Don't mind if I do. Gin and tonic. Large."

Humming, O'Rourke hung Trumper's coat in the closet and poured gin and tonic for both of them.

Drink in hand, Trumper made himself comfortable in the deep chair he always favored. "Did you talk to Gillian?"

"She wasn't at home. It's just us."

"Oh." Trumper didn't seem disappointed.

O'Rourke lit a cigarette and sipped his own drink. Every thing was perfect, he thought.

He told Trumper about the Casino in Baden-Baden. Mos elegant place he'd ever seen. Like a bloody palace. The club in London were nothing by comparison. But the Germa people left something to be desired. Heavy drinkers and ver officious. Always sticking their noses into other people's busi ness and telling them what to do.

"Is that a fact?"

"One woman came up to me and kicked up a frightfu row because I was smoking."

"Really? What did you do, Ken?"

"Told her to shut up."

Trumper nodded approvingly. O'Rourke went on to de scribe the sex shop in Karlsruhe. Definitely inferior. The he brought out some of the magazines he'd been looking a earlier. He perched on the arm of Trumper's chair, and the leafed through a few. Trumper's opinion was that *Bound anc Beaten* was the better magazine, but that when all was saic and done neither was as good as *Teenage Discipline*.

O'Rourke refilled Trumper's glass. Then he took the pack age Trumper had brought him and went into the bathroom.

When he returned, the syringe had one hundred milligrams of the anesthetic in it.

Trumper had put his glass on the table beside his chair and was absorbed in one of the magazines. Hearing O'Rourke, he looked up. His eyes widened when he saw the syringe. "What've you got there?"

O'Rourke quickly stepped in front of the chair and when Trumper tried to get up, he pushed him down.

"No!" Trumper gasped. "Please, Ken, don't! I'm clean now. I don't want—" He made another attempt to get up.

O'Rourke shoved him backward and gripped his wrist.

"No!" Trumper yelled, pulling his wrist free. "No!" He

icked O'Rourke in the leg. O'Rourke almost dropped the syringe.

"Hold still, stupid," O'Rourke said. "This isn't going to hurt you. I just have to find out."

But Trumper was panic-stricken. He hit at O'Rourke's arm again and gave him another kick in the leg.

O'Rourke swore and once more grabbed Trumper's wrist. Trumper writhed and made an attempt to roll sideways over the arm of the chair. The glass with the gin and tonic fell to the floor. O'Rourke put the syringe on the table and seized Trumper's other arm. "Stop it, you bloody fool! This isn't going to hurt you."

Trumper continued to struggle. Fear gave him added strength. Panting and grunting, he twisted and turned in the chair and beat the floor with his heels. O'Rourke lost his patience. He jammed his knee into Trumper's stomach and pinned him against the back of the chair with his forearm. Trumper squealed. O'Rourke reached for the syringe, then shifted his position and held Trumper against the back of the chair with his shoulder. Trumper uttered another squeal. O'Rourke forced Trumper's hand to the arm of the chair and found the vein. He stuck the needle into it.

Trumper let out a yell. O'Rourke pushed down on the plunger.

Within seconds, Trumper was unconscious.

O'Rourke released him and glanced at his watch. Trumper had slid sideways in the chair, his head resting on his shoulder. O'Rourke brought over an ottoman and put Trumper's feet on it. The feet were surprisingly heavy. Then he placed Trumper in a less awkward position and studied him. His jaw was slack, but he was breathing evenly and appeared to be comfortable.

O'Rourke took the syringe into the bathroom and cleaned it carefully. He'd confirmed one of his suspicions. An injection into the vein was far more difficult to administer than an injection into the muscle. It could be impossible, with a man who was strong and offering resistance from a standing position.

He went back to the lounge, wiped up the spilled drink and turned the pages of the magazine, pausing from time to time to study the sleeping Trumper. Once he went over to him and slapped him hard across the face. Trumper's head moved, but there was no other reaction. O'Rourke sat down again and devoted himself to the magazine.

Finally Trumper's eyelids began to flutter. He moaned. Then he opened his eyes.

O'Rourke looked at his watch. Twenty-six minutes.

Trumper closed his eyes, opened them, closed them and opened them. "Where am I?" he asked, puzzled.

"With me."

"Ken?"

"None other."

"What am I doing here?"

"You were asleep."

Trumper tried to get out of the chair, but seemed to lack the energy.

"Relax," O'Rourke said. "There's no hurry."

Trumper closed his eyes, but presently he began to shiver. The shivering grew worse. His teeth chattered. A moment later he was whimpering. A tear slid down his cheek.

O'Rourke got up and went to the chair in which Trumper was slumped, hugging himself and sobbing. O'Rourke put his arms around him and held him. The shivering, he decided, was to be expected.

"Don't worry," he said soothingly. "You're going to be all right. I had to find out, though."

Trumper rested his head against O'Rourke's chest. "My hand hurts."

"It'll be all right."

"I'm cold."

"You'll soon be warm."

Trumper looked up at him. His eyes were filled with tears. "Did you do something to me?"

"I gave you a little shot. Like the doctor gives you. I didn't hurt you, Trump."

Trumper seemed to be recollecting. He tried to draw away. O'Rourke's arms tightened around him.

"Don't be afraid," O'Rourke said. "I won't do it again, I promise. I simply had to find out. Here, let's unbutton your shirt and make you comfortable." He worked at the buttons.

Trumper struggled feebly for a few moments, then gave up and let himself be undressed.

24

Ranken was seated at a table by himself in the hotel bar when Ganzhorn found him. His expression was morose.

Ganzhorn sat down heavily at the same table. His expression was equally morose.

"Any progress?" Ranken asked.

Ganzhorn shook his head. "They tell you nothing, the police. They just ask more questions. They are investigating, they say. That is all. Investigating."

Ranken sighed. The past forty hours had been most unpleasant. Ganzhorn had received a certain amount of sympathy from their co-workers, but he himself hadn't. Everyone seemed to feel that he'd contributed to the theft by making friends with a stranger, and he couldn't help but agree with them. If the Englishman had actually been the thief, that is. The police were skeptical. The car, according to the police, could have been stolen by anyone.

But there was no doubt in Ganzhorn's mind. The Englishman had stolen the car keys and parking ticket when he'd gone back to the cloakroom. Then he'd simply driven the car out of the garage and taken off for some unknown destination. Ranken was of the same opinion, although he tried not to be. And Werben, to the extent that he could remember anything at all of the evening, was quite sure that he hadn't trusted the man from the beginning.

The members of the firm had had their farewell dinner at the Europäischer Hof the evening before, and the theft of Ganzhorn's car had been the main topic of conversation. Everyone had had a different thought on the matter. But there had been unanimity on one point: it was unlikely that Ganzhorn would ever see the car again.

And the police, while they hadn't actually said so, implied that the chances of locating it were slim. It was probable, they said, that the car had been driven immediately to another country, repainted, given new registration plates and had the serial numbers filed off. Car thieves operated on an international basis and were highly skilled at their work. Professional car thieves, at any rate. The police couldn't rule out the possibility that Ganzhorn's car had been stolen by an amateur.

Ranken's private belief was that if the Englishman had indeed stolen the car, he was just that—an amateur. Simply because he couldn't conceive of any member of a ring of car thieves dressing as the Englishman had been dressed. And because he couldn't conceive of a professional car thief stealing a three-year-old car that had sixty-five thousand kilometers showing on the speedometer.

"A beer?" he suggested.

Ganzhorn shrugged.

Ranken went over to the bar and ordered a beer for Ganzhorn and a second beer for himself. He carried them to the table. "Have they questioned anyone at the airport?" he asked as he resumed his seat.

Ganzhorn nodded. "No private plane from Geneva landed on Thursday."

Aha, thought Ranken.

"They have checked the applications at the Casino, also," Ganzhorn added. "There were several forms filled out by Britishers. Not too many. One of the attendants who was on duty remembers someone who answers Howard's description, but doesn't know which application was his."

"And the name—?"

"There was no application form from anyone with the name of James Howard."

"So it was a false name," Ranken said. His gloom escalated. He *had* been a fool.

"They have taken the names and passport numbers of the Britishers and are comparing them with hotel records," Ganzhorn said. "But even if they find the hotel the man stayed at—what does that prove? A man arrived and left and meanwhile went to the Casino. We have no photograph. We have no evidence. All we know is that an Englishman lied about being flown here from Geneva and lied about his name and we drove him to the Casino in my car."

Ranken reviewed the questions the Englishman had put to him on the train. They too were evidence of a sort. But they were no more conclusive evidence than the fact that the man had been untruthful and had disappeared from the Casino without saying that he intended to leave.

Ganzhorn sipped his beer. "What I don't understand is, if it was the Englishman, why did he choose my car? True, it was in good condition. But it was not new. It was not worth as much as many of the other cars in the garage at the time. Of course—" he regarded Ranken balefully—"you were the one he made friends with on the train, and through you he was introduced to me."

Ranken looked away. Professional car thieves, he thought, didn't need introductions to the individuals whose cars they

tended to steal. They knew how to open locks and start
engines without keys. And many of them had keys that made
lock-picking unnecessary. "What is the opinion of the police
about that?" he asked.

"They merely speculate. The man may have taken my car
simply because it attracted his attention for some reason. Or
because he didn't intend to resell it—he needed a car for
some particular purpose."

"But what purpose could he have had?"

"To use it in committing another crime."

Ranken suppressed a groan.

Neither of them spoke for a while. Ranken had already
decided to leave Baden-Baden a day sooner than he'd planned.
Now he considered leaving that very evening. The trip had
been spoiled for him, as it had been for Ganzhorn. The remain-
der of his stay was bound to be unpleasant.

He drank his beer slowly. It would be wonderful if the
police found the car while he was still in the city and if no
damage had been done to it. These possibilities existed. He
couldn't quite convince himself, however, that the odds were
very good.

His imagination veered off in a different direction. Could
Howard, or whatever his real name was, be a member of a
terrorist gang? Could he be planning to use the car in a bank
robbery or a kidnaping attempt?

He shuddered.

The man hadn't looked like a terrorist. On the other hand,
terrorists never looked like what they were. That was why
they were able to get away with the things they did.

He made an effort to control his imaginings. The man
was no terrorist. A criminal, perhaps. A minor criminal. One
who, sooner or later, would be caught.

"If the police believe that the Englishman is the primary
suspect," he asked, "what will they do?"

"They didn't say," Ganzhorn replied. "They have their

methods, I suppose. They will notify the authorities in England. Perhaps Interpol, as well. But that will not bring my car back."

"It might," Ranken said without conviction.

Ganzhorn didn't bother to comment.

Ranken finished his beer. He was reluctant to remain in Ganzhorn's company any longer; being with Ganzhorn only made him feel worse.

The telephone rang. The bartender answered it. A moment later he came out from behind the bar and approached their table.

"Is either of you gentlemen Mr. Heinz Ganzhorn?" he asked.

"I am," Ganzhorn said.

"There is a telephone call for you. You can take it at the telephone in the reception hall."

Ganzhorn got up from the table and left the room.

He was gone for some minutes.

His expression, when he returned, was no more cheerful than it had been before.

"That was the police," he said. "They have found a car with my license plates, but it is not my car. It is a Ford Fiesta and it belongs to a man from Köln. He was at the Casino on Thursday." He sat down. "It would seem that your friend Howard was even more clever than we thought." His face darkened. His frown deepened. "I wonder what he could be planning."

25

Hand in hand, Cochran and Ruth followed the porter into Heathrow's Number Two Terminal. Neither of them spoke. They had had little to say for the past thirty minutes, since leaving the Basil Street Hotel. After telling the taxi driver where to take them, Cochran had lapsed into a self-absorbed silence, and Ruth, after two halfhearted attempts to start a conversation, had given up and turned away to gaze out the window.

His expression was grim. Hers was pensive.

The lobby was crowded, and there was a long queue at the check-in counter. The porter deposited Ruth's luggage at the base of the counter. Cochran paid him, then took Ruth's hand again and stood beside her as she waited her turn. He didn't release the hand until she needed it to reach into her pocketbook for her ticket and passport. At that point he put her luggage on the scale and moved away to watch

her complete the transaction that would take her out of h
life.

He felt like a condemned man advancing into the executi
yard. He'd known that the end was near. Now he was with
minutes of it.

Clutching her boarding pass and embarkation card, Rut
joined him.

"All set?" he asked.

"All set," she replied.

"There's time for a drink."

"O.K."

They rode the escalator to the departure level and foun
a table.

"What'll it be?" he asked.

"It doesn't matter. Scotch, I guess."

He went to the bar and ordered two Scotches, then carrie
them back to the table. Ruth was filling out her embarkatio
card. She finished and put it under her pocketbook. He gav
her one of the drinks.

"I *will* call you tomorrow," she said as he sat down.

"I wish you wouldn't." They'd had the same discussio
earlier, when they were still in bed.

"You're being very foolish, John. You're—you're—I don'
know—it's as if—"

"I'm deliberately trying to self-destruct. You've already tol
me that." He gulped some Scotch. "Well, I'm not. You hav
a career, a life. I'm not good for you. I'm not even goo
for myself."

"The least I could do is get in touch with Todd. We coul
find *out.*"

He shrugged. It was a gesture not of indifference but o
hopelessness.

"I don't give up easily, John." She forced a smile. "I stucl
it out with Charlie for twelve years."

"And where did it get you?"

She managed to keep the smile going. "To Europe."

"You're the one who's trying to self-destruct." He finished his drink.

Her smile faded. "In other words, this is it. We met, we had four days together, and now we forget the whole thing. Is that what you're telling me?"

He said nothing.

She picked up her drink and drank it all at once. It was the first time he'd seen her do that, and he was startled. Her face flushed, she put the glass down sharply and said, "All right, I won't call. But I'll give you my addresses, in case you change your mind." She tore the flap from the ticket envelope and began to write.

"Ruth," he said, and found that his voice had become hoarse. He cleared his throat.

She finished writing and pushed the flap across the table. "There. I'll be with Beatrix until the twenty-seventh. After that I'll be in Munich. You have both addresses. Sooner or later, you may decide to use one of them."

"Ruth," he said, and cleared his throat again. "It's not that I don't care." He put the addresses into his pocket.

"I *know* that. It's just that you've hated yourself for so long, that you've—you've . . . This is silly, John, prolonging these last few minutes. We'll spoil everything. My plane leaves in half an hour. I'm going to go." She gathered her documents and pocketbook and got up. "Goodbye, John. I do love you, you know." She hurried from the table and along the corridor to the passport-control area.

He watched her and saw the distance between them increase. He had a wild desire to jump up and run after her. He didn't give in to it, however. He remained in his chair, gripping the edge of the table, his knuckles white, his teeth clenched, until he was sure she'd gone through passport control and entered the departure lounge. Then he released the table, pushed his chair back and got to his feet.

When he passed the entrance to the departure lounge he averted his eyes. He strode briskly to the stairway, descended to the ground level, continued across the check-in area and left the building.

It was time, he told himself, to go back to being John Cochran.

But that night, for the first time since the evening in Soho when he'd agreed to work for David Arlen, he took a long walk. He had no destination in mind when he left the flat. He simply walked. South, west, north, then back to his starting point. He covered eighteen miles.

26

O'Rourke finished his explanation.

Garwood stared at his empty teacup. His expression revealed nothing. Finally he said, "What time do you estimate you'll be in Amsterdam?"

"Depends," O'Rourke replied. "Driving should take an hour and a half to an hour and three quarters. It's a narrow road from the Hook of Holland to the motorway, and you have to follow it almost to Rotterdam. But once you're on the motorway, it's a piece of cake. It depends, though, what time he gets off the boat and all." He paused to reflect. "Ten thirty at the latest, I'd say. Nine thirty at the earliest."

Garwood nodded thoughtfully. "You know your way around Amsterdam?"

"Didn't get there," O'Rourke said tersely.

"You'll need a map, then."

O'Rourke shrugged one shoulder indifferently. "I'll leave the car in the outskirts. I'll take a taxi."

Garwood appeared to be weighing the matter.

O'Rourke watched him. Where's my money? he thoug[

"The airport car-park would be the best place to leave i
Garwood said. "It would give the impression . . . But y
might have difficulty finding the airport. . . . I daresay
matters not where you leave the car."

Matters not, thought O'Rourke. Like a bloody poet. Wl
about my money, you bastard?

"Very well," Garwood concluded. "Your plan sounds r
sonable. I suggest, however, that you drive a sufficient distan
into the city so that you'll have no difficulty in getting
taxi."

"Naturally."

"I'll be at the Hilton. I'll wait for you in the lobby. I
expect you no later than eleven o'clock. If you're not the
by then—" His voice trailed off.

"If I'm not there by then?" O'Rourke prodded.

"I'll notify the police."

O'Rourke opened a fresh packet of cigarettes, tapped t[
packet lightly against his hand until a cigarette popped u
then took it from the packet and lit it. He performed ea[
step of the little operation with great deliberation, as if l
were concerned with nothing else. He was determined n[
to show the anger that was sweeping over him. He blew
cloud of smoke at Garwood's face and smiled lazily. "Is th
so?"

"It is so. For a period of approximately two hours y[
will be in possession of a large amount of money. I feel
only fair to warn you that should you surrender to the perfect
human temptation to keep any or all of it, you'll be arreste[
Those arrangements I will make. Believe me."

"Is that so?"

"Quite definitely." Garwood permitted himself to smil[
It wasn't a pleasant smile, because his eyes weren't include[
in it. "Of course," he said, "I'm certain that this portion [

ur conversation is most unnecessary. If I'd had any doubts bout you, I wouldn't have contacted you in the first place."

O'Rourke was appeased, but only slightly. "I'm glad to ear you say that. Now what about my money?"

Garwood nodded. "I have it." He made no move to hand t over, however. "By and large," he said, "I think you've done quite well. Your plan is not one that I myself would ave thought of, but I must say it strikes me as sound. I would have preferred to take possession of the money somewhere in Switzerland, and I'm not altogether sure that I approve of the use of an automobile, but I gather that you have your reasons."

More of the anger vanished. "Naturally I have my reasons. I can't order the bloody trains to leave exactly when I want them to."

This time Garwood's smile was more genuine. "No, I daresay you can't."

"My money," O'Rourke reminded him.

Garwood reached into the scuffed leather portfolio he was holding on his lap and removed a large brown manila envelope. It was sealed, but it appeared to be quite full. He put it on the table. "Fifteen hundred," he said. "Also your tickets, and another three hundred for expenses."

O'Rourke glanced around. They were alone. He listened. There were no footsteps on the stairs. He took the envelope, slit it open at the top and peered inside. He made no attempt to count the money, though. This wasn't the place for that.

"It's all there," Garwood assured him.

"I should hope so," he replied. He put the envelope on his lap. "There are a few extras you'll have to pay for, though."

"Oh?"

O'Rourke decided to round off the amount. "Four hundred pounds, to be exact."

"Oh? What items are you referring to, may I ask?"

"The drug. My suit. A shirt."

"Your suit? A shirt?" Garwood's expression was one of amazement.

"I tore a perfectly good new suit and ruined a very nice shirt."

Garwood's lips twitched. "Astonishing," he said. But then he frowned. "How did these misfortunes occur?"

"On the car door," O'Rourke said easily.

Garwood's lips twitched again. "Incredible." He took a deep breath. "Very well. I'll reimburse you. In Amsterdam."

O'Rourke nodded his assent. His anger was completely gone now. The lawyer was, if nothing else, reasonable.

"But let's get on with more important matters," Garwood said. "You don't as yet have any idea what Cochran looks like."

"I was meaning to ask you about that."

"I think we'd best take a little walk."

"A walk?" O'Rourke looked perplexed. "Where to?"

"Not far. I'll show you."

O'Rourke thought of the envelope he was holding and grew suspicious. "I don't want to take a walk. Besides, there's another matter that needs to be settled."

Garwood's eyebrows rose. "There is? Not a new pair of shoes, I hope."

O'Rourke shook his head. "My accommodation on the bloody ship. They have better cabins than the shoebox you got me the last time. I want one."

"Impossible," Garwood said. "You have a cabin adjoining Cochran's."

O'Rourke's eyes widened in surprise. "I do? How do you know?"

"From an informer."

This time O'Rourke wasn't satisfied by that explanation. "What informer? How did you find out what cabin Cochran has? You know more than you've told me. I don't like it."

"It's quite simple. The agent from whom Cochran buys

is tickets is an acquaintance of an acquaintance of mine."
He winked. "And he's a susceptible young man."

O'Rourke considered. It was possible, he supposed. But
doubt lingered. "How did you meet him?"

"I didn't meet him. I have no intention of meeting him.
The person who told me about Cochran having the money
and taking it to Switzerland also told me about the travel
agent. And, I might add, made the arrangements."

"Then he's not an acquaintance."

"Let's not sit here discussing semantic differences. We have
more important things to go over. Come with me."

O'Rourke hesitated.

"It isn't wise for us to remain here," Garwood said. "It's
almost time for the luncheon crowd, which is usually considerable. One never knows whom one might meet."

"True," O'Rourke admitted, although he didn't think that
anyone they met would recognize him. The people he knew
didn't frequent second-rate sandwich bars in the vicinity of
the Royal Courts of Justice—not unless they were in serious
trouble. "Very well."

They got up and went down the staircase to the ground
floor. Garwood was right, O'Rourke conceded. A number of
people were standing at the counter, waiting for sandwiches.
The dining room would soon be filled.

"This way," Garwood said, turning left on Chancery Lane.

O'Rourke followed reluctantly. The narrow street was
crowded. Automobiles and pedestrians alike seemed to be in
a hurry. O'Rourke clutched the envelope under his arm. Soon
he relaxed, however, for no one was paying any attention to
him.

They came to Carey Street. "We cross here," Garwood
said. But the traffic was heavy, and they had to wait. "A
thought occurs to me," Garwood said. "It would help, at
the moment of your—shall we say—meeting with Cochran
if you said something to put him off his guard."

O'Rourke threw him a quick glance.

"I suggest you say—should you find it necessary, that is—that you have a message for him from Peter Evans, or mention Peter Evans in some way."

"Peter Evans?"

"That's a friend of his. It will tend to, I believe, authenticate you."

"Peter Evans," O'Rourke repeated. "Peter Evans."

There was an opening in the traffic. "Come," Garwood said.

They crossed Chancery Lane and entered Carey Street. On their right were the facades of the buildings that housed the lawyers' offices; on their left, across the street the massive complex of the Royal Courts of Justice. After a short distance they came to an arcade that led from Carey Street into New Square. "This way," Garwood said, leading O'Rourke into the arcade. Halfway through it, he stopped. "Tomorrow, at two o'clock, I want you to be standing exactly here."

O'Rourke looked around. A heavy wooden gate with iron studs in it and a crown of iron spikes stood open. A porter's trolley stood against one wall. The wall was hung with caricatures of bewigged judges and other figures that appeared to belong to the legal profession. Set into the opposite wall were the door and display windows of a shop that sold lawbooks.

"Where are we?" he asked.

Garwood ignored the question. "Tomorrow, at two o'clock or a few minutes after two o'clock, I shall come through this passageway from that direction with another gentleman. I shall say goodbye to him here and return the way I came. He will continue to the street there and, most likely, hail a taxi. I want you to take a good look at him. He will go directly from here to meet John Cochran."

O'Rourke nodded his quick comprehension. The informer. "Ah. And you want me to follow him."

"That won't be necessary. They'll meet at two thirty in

e buffet at Victoria Air Terminal. You be there too. In at way you'll see Cochran. What you do after that is up you. He'll be on Wednesday evening's Sealink steamer to olland, as will you. . . . Is everything understood?"

"Couldn't be more so," O'Rourke replied. You had to give e lawyer credit, he thought; the man was a planner.

"Excellent. I'll leave you, then. We'll meet in the lobby the Hilton in Amsterdam on Thursday." He paused. "And meant every word I said."

O'Rourke smiled. He suddenly felt good. At last he was ing to set eyes on the smuggler. "Don't worry," he said eerfully, "it's not just anybody you're dealing with. It's Ken- eth O'Rourke."

"That it is," said Garwood. He turned abruptly and went rough the passageway into New Square.

Humming, and with the envelope under his arm, O'Rourke traced his steps to Carey Street. It was time for lunch, d he intended to eat at one of the better places. Possibly e Savoy.

Garwood settled back in his chair and laced his fingers. e could understand the need for a car. He could understand 'Rourke's unwillingness to show the identification required hire one. It was even possible that O'Rourke carried no edit cards. Yet the idea of the stolen car sitting in the ar-park outside the terminal at the Hook of Holland troubled im.

On the other hand, when it came to motor cars, O'Rourke ad an excellent reputation. If he said the car was disguised, t undoubtedly was.

A torn suit. A ruined shirt. It was almost comical. Better pay, however. Psychopaths were unpredictable. Big things idn't bother them, but little things did. And O'Rourke obvi- usly had a bad temper.

Switzerland would have been better than Holland. There

was nothing wrong with Holland, though. And O'Rourke ha
shown considerable ingenuity. Really, when you stopped t
think about it . . .

Garwood unlaced his fingers and reached for the telephon
Peter Evans answered after the first ring.

27

The kitchen brought back memories of the mornings with Ruth, so Cochran took his coffee into the lounge and drank it standing at the window, gazing at the Basil Street Hotel, which also brought back memories of Ruth.

His back and legs ached. He was no longer used to walking for seven consecutive hours. Yet he had an urge to go out and take another walk. He was determined not to give in to it, however. His robot days were over. Never again would he wind himself up and turn himself loose on the streets of London. Last night was the final time.

He left the window, sank painfully into a deep chair and finished his coffee. He forced himself to think of other matters.

Wednesday night, Garwood had said, and Wednesday's date was stamped on the ticket. Evans would be in touch with him a day or two before. . . . Somewhere in England an old lady was dying, and her son was looking toward a comfortable future in a foreign land. . . . The last of a dwindling fortune. How long had the fortune been in the hands of the Evans family? Centuries, perhaps.

That had been one of the causes of Europe's troubles, Ru
had said. Money had stayed in the same families too lon
Well, things were certainly different now. To avoid beir
stripped by taxes, people with money were being forced
hide it, to go into exile. If money was freedom, freedom
last bastion was the Swiss bank.

But freedom no longer meant what it had once mean
Freedom today meant a four-room condominium on the Cost
del Sol and a communal swimming pool. Ardmore Properti
sold freedom. And John Cochran was freedom's courier.

He sighed and carried the empty cup into the kitcher
where he washed it, dried it, put it back on the shelf. The
he went into the bedroom. The scent of Ruth seemed t
hover over everything. He looked at the items on the dresse
His wallet, some loose change, a handkerchief, the comb an
hairbrush Ruth had used, the flap of the ticket envelope she'
given him.

Beatrix Coertsen, 74 Reijnier Vinkeles Kade.

God, how he wanted to pick up the telephone and cal

He crumpled the flap of the ticket envelope and threw i
into the wastebasket.

74 Reijnier Vinkeles Kade. He would remember the addres
for the rest of his life. Also the address in Munich. But h
would never use either one.

He fished the wad of paper from the wastebasket an
smoothed it out, then threw it away again and went int
the bathroom. A hot bath was what he needed. A long ho
bath would ease his sore muscles. He turned on the wate
in the tub.

The telephone rang, and his heart lurched. She'd ignorec
his request and was calling from Amsterdam.

He raced into the bedroom.

But it was Kitty. "I thought you might like to have dinner
with us this evening," she said.

She was being kind, he knew. No doubt she was also curious,

though. And he didn't feel up to coping with either kindness or curiosity. "That's very nice of you," he said, "and normally I'd be glad to. But I'm getting ready to go away for a few days."

"Oh?"

He could guess her thoughts: he was preparing to follow Ruth to Holland. "To Spain," he said. In the past he'd given Spain as his destination when he'd had to go to Geneva.

"Oh." She sounded disappointed.

"Another time," he said. "I'll only be gone a few days."

She said nothing, but he imagined the questions that were running through her mind. "I'll call you when I get back," he said quickly, "and we'll get together then." He put down the telephone.

The hot water did ease the soreness in his back and legs. It didn't do much for his spirits, however. He had to get out of the flat, he decided. That's all there was to it. He had to get out of the flat. A few drinks and some lunch at a pub would take care of two hours or so. Then maybe a movie. He hadn't been to a movie in months.

He went to the Crown and Sceptre and stayed there until after two o'clock. But he didn't go to a movie. The need to take a walk got the better of him. He walked west and north across Kensington into Bayswater and across Bayswater to the southern fringe of Paddington. He stopped finally at the church of St. Stephen the Martyr, on Westbourne Park Road. He recalled having paused at St. Stephen's on two occasions during the months of despair following Stephanie's death, to rest. The name was what had attracted his attention. Both times he'd found the building unheated and unlit. But sitting in one of the back pews, hugging himself for warmth and gazing through the half-darkness at the altar of the dreary old church which even in its best days had probably not had a prosperous congregation, he'd felt some of the weariness leave him and he'd experienced a few minutes of peace.

Now he found the doors locked, however.

Too tired to walk back to his flat, he took a taxi.

He was hanging up his coat when the telephone rang. Ruth?

His hopes rose and fell.

"Mr. Cochran?"

He recognized the voice immediately. "Yes."

"Mr. *John* Cochran?"

"Yes, Evans."

"You—you've been out?"

"Yes."

"I thought so. I've been ringing for—er—some little time." Cochran said nothing.

"I—er—want to arrange to turn the money over to you I—er—"

"O.K. Arrange."

"Well, I thought tomorrow afternoon. Two thirty, I thought. At, if you don't mind, the same place we—er—met before. The buffet at Victoria Air Terminal. Unless, that is—"

Cochran sighed. Events did have their own momentum. "Very well. Two thirty, Victoria Air Terminal."

"The buffet."

"The buffet."

Cochran hung up and seated himself on the bed. He thought of the new suitcase, still in the box, in his closet. He saw himself boarding the ship. He saw himself carrying the suitcase through the Gare de Cornavin in Geneva. He saw himself depositing three thousand pounds in his account at the Union Bank of Switzerland on the Rue du Rhône. None of the mental pictures particularly cheered him.

Yet, somehow, he did feel better. It was as if the call from Evans had accomplished what the walk had failed to accomplish. It had given him a new sense of himself. He was John Cochran, and John Cochran had a job to do, the sort of job he was good at.

28

Evans was already there. He was seated at a table near the cashier's station. He looked pale and worried.

Cochran dropped onto the chair facing him, but said nothing.

Evans heaved an audible sigh of relief. His lips twitched. It was as if he wanted to smile but was afraid that something terrible would happen to his face if he did. His hands were clasped tightly on the blue-and-white checked tablecloth.

Cochran waited.

"I—er—have the money," Evans said in a tight voice.

Cochran nodded. He could understand Evans's anxiety. This was all the money Evans had in the world, and all he ever hoped to have. He was about to turn it over to a man who was virtually a stranger. Cochran felt sorry for him.

"It—it's in the left-luggage room."

"You have the claim check?"

Evans unclasped his hands. It seemed to be an effort for

him to get them apart. He reached into the pocket of his topcoat and took out the receipt, then put it on the table, all in slow motion. "A—a pigskin at-at-attaché c-case," he said, beginning to stutter.

"Relax," Cochran said, and put the slip of paper into the pocket of his leather jacket.

Again Evans's lips twitched. Apparently he wanted to relax but he simply couldn't. Cochran guessed that the next two days were going to be hell for Evans.

"I—you—you l-leave tomorrow n-n-night?" Evans asked.

"How's your mother?" Cochran asked.

Evans blinked rapidly. "You know?"

"Your uncle told me."

"He's not really my uncle. He—I just call him that. I have ever since I was a child. He—he was a friend of my father's." He'd stopped stuttering, Cochran noted, and returned to stammering. "My mother's—not at all well. She—she's—er—in hospital. I'm afraid—well, I'm anxious to get back from Switzerland as soon as possible. You—er—understand."

"I understand."

"I—er—I wanted to travel *with* you," Evans went on. "On the same train, that is. But Uncle Michael didn't think it would be, well, wise."

Cochran felt another brief pang of sympathy. "He wouldn't have picked me if he hadn't thought I was trustworthy."

This time Evans actually did manage to smile. His expression was one of gratitude. "I—appreciate what you're doing."

"I'm getting paid for it."

"Of course. But, still." He paused. "I—I'm not very good at, well, earning a living."

Cochran was startled by the confession. "Have you ever tried?"

"Yes, several times. I—I worked. I—it wasn't very—er—satisfactory."

Cochran grinned. He wanted to say, "Shut up before I

art liking you." He didn't say it, though. "You married?" he asked instead.

Evans shook his head.

Cochran returned to the original question. "Yes, I leave tomorrow night. I'll arrive in Geneva Thursday evening. The train gets in around a quarter to seven."

"I was married once," Evans said, "but my wife and my mother . . . A quarter to seven? Yes, I know. I'll be there."

"At the *station?*"

"Well—er—no, not at the station. I mean, Uncle Michael—er—pointed out that the banks will be, well, closed at that time. I'll be at the—er—hotel. I've booked a room at the Richemond. You—er—know where it is?"

"Rue des Alpes, isn't it?"

Evans looked pleased. "Exactly. Rue des Alpes. I—I was in Geneva once, many years ago. I'm afraid I don't remember it very well."

"I'm there quite often."

"Yes, I daresay you are. I've booked the room for tomorrow night and Thursday night. I'm flying down tomorrow. I thought—that is, well, you never know about the weather. I mean, on Thursday there might be fog or, well, almost anything. So I discussed it with Uncle Michael, and he approved. Of my going tomorrow, that is."

"Do you discuss *everything* with your Uncle Michael?"

Evans sensed criticism and looked hurt. "No, naturally not. Not everything. But, well, when it comes to—er—financial matters—well, you see, he and my father were great chums, and my mother—well, my mother had great—how shall I put it?—great confidence in him. He—he's managed the assets since my father's death. Since before my father's death, actually. He's even an Authorized Depository."

"So he told me."

"Then you understand."

"Not entirely."

"The—er—assets have been in his hands. Like, well, a bank. He's managed them."

"And he's done a good job?"

"Oh, quite. I mean, the best he could. There wasn't much he could do. Until now, that is. I mean, he had to sell them. In order for me to have the cash, you understand." Involuntarily, Evans glanced in the direction of the left-luggage room. "Most of the estate has been—well, in land and Hastings Gate Priory."

"Hastings Gate Priory?"

"Our house."

"Oh."

"The bonds—well, you know. He's been selling them gradually, poor man, so that we'd have the wherewithal to live. Now, unfortunately—or fortunately—he found a buyer for the house. An Arab from Kuwait. I'll be comfortable enough. But poor Uncle Michael . . ." He didn't finish.

Cochran studied him. The tension was gone. To the extent, Cochran supposed, that it was ever gone. He was beginning to suspect that Evans had never in his life been entirely free of anxiety. *"Poor* Uncle Michael?"

Evans nodded. "It isn't easy for him. You see, well, at one time he was—what shall I say?—an important figure. He had a large number of wealthy clients. But so many have died—it was a different—er—generation, don't you know. Now everything is, well, corporations and big businessmen and people who fly here and there in jets. It—it isn't his world any longer. He doesn't, well, complain, but I know how it must be. And since his wife died—Aunt Penny, that is—he's been quite alone. He's let himself go. Rather dreadfully, I'm afraid. He isn't the same man. Not at all—er—the same man. You—you didn't know him before. He's let himself become—well, you've met him. What's your opinion?"

Cochran withheld his opinion. He recalled the frayed

sweater. But he also recalled the coldness, the arrogance. Was it possible that Garwood was a predator who had lost his teeth? It didn't really matter. All that mattered was that Michael Garwood, whatever he was, had a certain power over John Cochran.

He shrugged, and his eyes wandered. The buffet was less crowded than it had been the first time he'd met Evans there. But this time too the patrons were mostly foreigners. People going back to their native countries to spend the holidays with their families. People going home.

He thought of Ruth.

"So you want me to bring the money to the hotel," he said harshly.

"I—if you would."

"I will. The train is hardly ever late. I should be at the Richemond between eight and eight thirty. Will you be registered under your own name?"

"Yes. I—" Evans broke off. His face clouded. "I never thought—I suppose I should have. It still isn't too late, I suppose. But then, they examine your passport when you register. I don't know. What do you advise?"

Ask Uncle Michael, Cochran thought. "It's unimportant," he said. "Leave things the way they are. I'll ask at the desk for Peter Evans."

Evans nodded. He began to look worried again. "You *will* be careful?"

"Cross my heart and hope to die."

"I beg your pardon?"

"Never mind. Yes, I'll be careful. For my own sake as well as yours."

Evans clasped his hands on the tablecloth again. He seemed to have nothing further to say, yet to be reluctant to leave.

"Any other questions?" Cochran asked.

"Er—no. You'll come to the hotel Thursday evening between eight and eight thirty?"

"Right."

Evans made a supreme effort and got up. "I—er—do thank you."

Cochran smiled reassuringly. "Don't worry."

Evans returned the smile bravely, then turned and walked away from the table.

Cochran remained seated for a moment, thinking. Evans had managed to give him an extraordinary sense of responsibility, and he needed time to shake it off. His ordinary sense of responsibility was more than enough.

At last he managed to dispatch Evans from his mind and left the buffet.

He walked casually across the smoking lounge, pushed the swinging door aside and presented himself at the left-luggage counter.

The attaché case was of tan pigskin and was large. It was even heavier than he'd imagined. The money, he guessed, was packed very tightly. There were, after all, seventeen thousand five hundred banknotes inside.

And, he knew, he was going to have to count every last one when he returned to his flat.

He descended the stairway to the main concourse and went outside. It was a clear afternoon, cool but not cold, and he'd walked from Basil Street to the air terminal. He would have liked to make the return trip on foot also. But the attaché case was too heavy.

He took the Victoria Line Underground to the Green Park station and transferred there to the Piccadilly Line. At three thirty he arrived at Knightsbridge and rode the escalator to the ground level. He left the Underground through the Sloane Street exit and turned toward Basil Street.

O'Rourke followed, humming all the way.

29

It had taken until four o'clock in the morning to count the money. But it had all been there. Three hundred and fifty-three thousand pounds.

Apparently Garwood felt sufficiently sure of him to pay him in advance.

He'd left the attaché case and the money on the table and gone to bed. He'd slept well, but he'd had an unpleasant dream. He'd dreamed about his grandmother. She'd been rebuking him. He'd tried to get away from her, but wherever he'd gone she'd followed him, her voice becoming increasingly strident. Finally she'd backed him into a corner from which there was no escape.

The dream had a certain validity. His grandmother had been a persistent, inflexible woman. He hadn't got along with her as well as he had with his grandfather. But she'd tempered her criticisms with kindness and she'd always tried to do the right thing by him. She'd never pursued him around the house with noisy, unrelenting reproaches.

Nevertheless, it was a relief to wake up and find that he hadn't been backed into a corner.

He glanced at his watch. A quarter to eleven. He rarely slept that late.

He made coffee and took it into the lounge. The attache case was as he'd left it, open, with some of the money inside and the rest stacked on the table. The sight of it reminded him that he had things to do.

He shaved, showered, dressed, then took the new suitcase from the carton and studied it. It was a large suit bag with three hangers, designed to be packed in an upright position, folded in the middle and fastened with two straps. He'd chosen it in preference to the ordinary box-type suitcase because it looked less like the sort of item that might have a false bottom and that the smugglers he'd encountered did use. And he still thought that the style was right. But suddenly he wasn't so sure about the color and material, bottle-green vinyl. In the store, they had seemed satisfactory. Dark enough, dull enough. But now, as he examined the bag from various angles, he wondered. Dark as it was, the vinyl appeared lustrous. By reflecting light, it called attention to itself.

I'm just jumpy, he decided. Customs officers don't examine a piece of luggage because of its luster. They don't think that way.

You never really knew, though. There was no such thing as really knowing.

Convinced, finally, that he'd been right in the first place and that the suitcase would do, he removed two of the hangers and hung a suit on the third. Then he rolled the money into shirts and underwear and stuffed it into the bottom of the case and around the suit. At first glance the bag would appear to contain one suit and a lot of laundry. By no means, he knew, would the money be adequately concealed in the event of an inspection; but, he also knew, there was no way in which such a large bulk could be concealed any better.

The important thing was to avoid inspection altogether.

When the new bag was packed, he took out the old suitcase that he normally used and filled it with enough clothes for a week's trip.

But at that point he had a crisis of nerve.

His entire plan began to seem wrong. It was unsafe to check a suitcase containing three hundred and fifty-three thousand pounds through from London to the Hook of Holland. It would pass through too many hands. Porters in London, at the quay in Harwich, on the ship, at the quay in Holland—any one of them could misdirect it. And the label specifying its destination could come off. Or the attendant at Liverpool Street Station could put the wrong label on at the very start. The whole idea was unwise.

He thought of Evans. The poor man was depending on him. He also thought of himself. If the suitcase was lost, Garwood would make sure that he was eventually arrested; he could count on that.

Then he began to consider the alternative. He pictured himself carrying two large suitcases, one filled with carelessly wrapped money. He pictured a customs agent approaching him. He heard the customs agent say, "I beg your pardon, sir, but would you be good enough to open those cases?"

He shuddered.

Those were the only options, though. He couldn't row the money across the goddamn North Sea. He either had to carry it with him or check it.

Suddenly, as if in a fit of temper, he grabbed his coat, picked up the suitcase with the money, hauled it down to the street and flagged a taxi. Checking the suitcase had seemed a good idea a week ago, and nothing had changed. Check it now, before you do something even more foolish.

He paid the taxi driver, carried the suitcase up the steps at the Liverpool Street Station to the Sealink office, gave the clerk one pound seventy-five, received his documents, took the suitcase downstairs to the Port-a-bag counter and handed it over with the documents.

"Tonight's Sealink to the Hook of Holland," he said.

The attendant took a paintbrush and put glue on the suitcase. Then he affixed a label. The label said, "HOOK OF HOLLAND." The number was A446. He gave the duplicate receipt to Cochran. The number on that was also A446.

Cochran left the Port-a-bag counter and strode to the entrance to the Underground.

He didn't know whether he'd done right or wrong; all he knew was that the matter was settled.

At ten minutes past three he returned to his flat.

O'Rourke watched him mount the steps and unlock the door to the lobby.

An ordinary type, he thought.

Cochran entered the building, and the door closed behind him.

O'Rourke continued his evaluation. It was the same evaluation he'd made the day before as he'd observed Cochran in the air terminal and in the Underground. Nothing special. Average height. A bit on the slender side—maybe eleven stone. Late thirties or early forties. Should be easy enough to handle.

On the basis of appearance, O'Rourke would have picked Evans as the smuggler and Cochran as the informer. For Evans had struck him as the smoother of the two men. Better dressed, better groomed, more professional-looking by far. But his nervous manner had given him away as the informer. Waiting for Cochran to arrive, he'd behaved like a man who was expecting at any moment to be assaulted.

In a physical contest with the American, O'Rourke mused, the advantage would lie with himself. First, there was the element of surprise—the American would be off guard. Second, there was the matter of age—the American was at least ten years older. As to physical strength, O'Rourke reserved judgment. Although the American outweighed him by perhaps a stone, there was nothing about him to suggest unusual strength. You couldn't be sure about something like that, though. People were always underestimating his own strength, O'Rourke knew. Because he was slight, they thought he was weak. They didn't realize until too late that he was like steel.

But then, he didn't intend that there would be a struggle. All he would have to do was carry the man, and he knew without any doubt that he was capable of carrying eleven stone of dead weight for a considerable distance.

He reached into the pocket of his suede coat and felt the weapon. It was a simple one: the wrench he'd bought in Germany, wrapped in an orlon sock. Everything he would need was in various pockets. For, while he had an aversion to wearing the same clothes two days in a row, he was traveling without luggage. He hadn't thought it wise to attempt to cope with Cochran *and* a suitcase. Besides, he'd be back in London within less than twenty-four hours.

He shifted his position. It was going to be a long and tiresome afternoon. He'd only arrived at two thirty, and already he was bored. But it had seemed prudent to begin his vigil early, for it was impossible to predict what steps Cochran might take to avoid being followed. He now knew what Cochran looked like, but he didn't know how Cochran's mind worked. It was safe to assume, though, that he was a slippery type.

He reached into the other pocket of his coat for his gloves. His hand encountered the syringe, the vial of Thiopental and the car keys. Then two other items.

He frowned. The two other items were the earrings he'd intended to give Gillian. He'd forgotten about them, but now they reminded him of the fact that he'd telephoned her no less than seven times since his return and she hadn't answered once. Unfaithful. No better than a whore, actually. He was going to have to take the matter up with her. He expected consideration, and she wasn't showing it. Perhaps he'd give the earrings to Janet. Janet wasn't much, but at least she was available when a chap needed her.

Putting on the gloves, he studied the building in which Cochran lived. It was nice enough in its way. So, for that matter, was the neighborhood. But it wasn't the sort of building or neighborhood to which O'Rourke aspired. Not sufficiently distinguished. Perhaps it was clever of Cochran to have picked this particular location, though, for it wasn't one in which you would expect a thief and smuggler to live. It was the sort of place in which you would expect to find dentists, architects and businessmen—those who were reasonably successful but not at the very top of the heap.

O'Rourke's thoughts drifted back to the air terminal. Interesting, the way in which Cochran had received the cloakroom ticket from the informer and taken the suitcase from the left-luggage room. Quite unoriginal. But then, the unoriginal enterprises were often the most successful. Interesting, too, that it was the informer who had given Cochran the cloakroom ticket. Evidently the informer was a confederate. So while Cochran was clever in some matters, he wasn't clever in others.

O'Rourke took a cigarette from one of the packets in the pocket of his jacket and lit it. He'd brought enough cigarettes for an extra day, just in case.

How much money was Cochran carrying? That was the question. There might be enough time in Holland to learn the answer.

Treasonous thoughts presented themselves to him. He resisted them. Garwood had warned him, and he could well believe that Garwood was not one to make idle threats.

Something to consider, though. Not to act on. Merely to consider.

But Trumper had warned him, too. Garwood was a man of influence, Trumper had said, Garwood had connections. Whatever else you do, don't double-cross Garwood.

Poor old Trump. A good sort, really. Just not very bright. Well . . .

He peeled back his glove and looked at his watch. Five minutes to four. Christ, the bloody minutes could drag.

By six o'clock he was thoroughly chilled and very angry. He'd spent three and a half hours in the sodding corridor between the Basil Street Hotel and the GLC Fire Brigade Station for nothing. Hooper's Court it was called. Hooper's Refuse Dump would have been more suitable. Only Kenneth O'Rourke would have put himself to such trouble. Only Kenneth O'Rourke would have anticipated that Cochran might do something unexpected.

Three thousand pounds wasn't enough. Not enough by half.

But suddenly he knew that he'd done the right thing. For at six o'clock, a full hour before he might have been expected to do so, the American emerged from the building O'Rourke had seen him enter. And he was carrying a suitcase. Not the suitcase he'd picked up at the air terminal. Another one.

Cochran turned into Hooper's Court and passed within three feet of him.

Smiling inwardly, O'Rourke followed.

Cochran went left at Brompton Road. At Hans Crescent, instead of entering the Underground, he waited for the traffic signal and crossed the street.

So did O'Rourke.

But then things went wrong. What O'Rourke had feared might happen, the one mishap he'd known he wouldn't be able to do anything about, did happen.

Cochran flagged a taxi that was heading east on Brompton Road, got in and was driven off.

And it took O'Rourke five minutes to get a taxi for himself.

"Liverpool Street Station," he told the driver. "As fast as you can."

But the driver was in no hurry. And it wouldn't have helped

matters if he had been, for every traffic light that could turn red did turn red, seconds before they reached it.

O'Rourke paid the driver, called him several names that left him open-mouthed with shock and ran into the terminal.

Cochran was nowhere in sight.

Waiting room, ticket office, Rainbow Buffet—there was no sign of him.

O'Rourke checked the entrances to the Underground. Without success.

He mingled with the passengers waiting at the gates. Nothing.

He crossed the taxi rank and inspected the platforms beyond it. Cochran wasn't on any of them.

O'Rourke entered the East End Buffet and the East End Bar, at the far end of the building. The American wasn't in either.

Enraged, O'Rourke returned to his starting point. The sodding bastard had given him the slip.

Then he realized that there was one place he hadn't searched. He climbed the steps.

And there was Cochran. Quietly having dinner by himself at a corner table in the Europa Bistro.

O'Rourke waited outside.

And at ten minutes to eight he followed Cochran into the train.

30

Tuesday had been a bad day for Ranken. He'd made his presentation, and the client had disapproved it. Not enough storage space, too much glass, and the stairway—well, the stairway was a disaster.

Ranken could agree that he might have skimped on the storage space; that could easily be remedied. And while he didn't really believe that there was too much glass, he was willing to give in on the point. But the stairway—that was a blow. It was the focal point of the ground-floor sales area, and the manner in which it branched to the left and right at the landing would improve the traffic flow on the first floor. The concept was taken from a stairway he'd seen and admired in Oslo, but he'd improved it and he knew it was right. He also knew that what the client really disapproved of wasn't the design but the price. The Swiss were miserly. They always had been.

Nevertheless he'd agreed to make changes and had stayed

up most of the night roughing them out, sketching a new plan for presentation at a second meeting, on Wednesday

But the client hadn't liked the revised plan any better than he'd liked the original. Ranken was going to have to start again from the beginning, and Mueller, his boss, was going to accuse him, as he had in the past, of being a poor salesman. "Any amateur can draw lines," he would say pointedly, "but it takes a professional to sell them."

The Wednesday meeting had lasted so long that he'd missed the flight he'd intended to take to Frankfurt. The flight he'd ended up taking had been delayed on the ground for an hour because of engine trouble, and then had been so rough that he'd spilled half a cup of coffee on himself.

Nothing had gone right. Nothing had gone right for an entire week.

Now, as the taxi pulled up in front of his house, he heaved a sigh of relief. A drink or two with his wife, a hot bath, a few minutes of good music would restore him. He didn't look forward to the following morning. He hoped that the office staff hadn't heard about the incident with the car in Baden-Baden, but he supposed they had. And Mueller was bound to show his displeasure over Zürich. The next few days would certainly be unpleasant. But if he was in the proper frame of mind he could get through them. And he was always in a better frame of mind when he was at home than when he was away. As a matter of fact, he thought as he put his key in the lock of the front door, he really didn't like traveling. He looked forward to a time when he wouldn't have to do it.

His wife had evidently heard the taxi. While he was still fiddling with the lock, she opened the door.

They embraced.

Children popped out of various rooms. He embraced them too.

"How was the trip?" his wife asked. She looked a bit worried.

"Don't ask," he replied. "Just pour me a drink."

He took off his coat and went into the living room. Two of the children followed him, competing to tell him of their doings. He loosened his tie.

His wife brought him a glass of his favorite cognac and shooed the children out of the room. Her expression was troubled. "Heinz wants you to call," she said.

"Ganzhorn? Did he tell you about the car? It was terrible. I met an Englishman on the train—"

"He sounded very upset. He'd been with the police. They want to talk to you also. I think you'd better call him."

Ranken's face lengthened. "Someone stole his car. Apparently they haven't found it. In a way it was my fault. I'll tell you about it later." He got up wearily and went to the telephone.

Ganzhorn was more than very upset. He was beside himself. The police had come for him in the middle of the afternoon. They'd detained him for four hours, at their headquarters in Hannover. The Frankfurt police would undoubtedly be around to question Ranken too. The matter had become more serious than either of them could have imagined. It was terrible. Who would have guessed?

"Calm yourself," Ranken told him. "What's so terrible? What's happened?"

"A woman has been murdered."

"A woman? Murdered?"

"A woman from Karlsruhe. An Erika Rebholz. She'd been missing since last Thursday. She was identified yesterday."

"Last Thursday?"

"They found her car in the underground garage in Karlsruhe. The license plates—it's complicated—the license plates, they've traced them back to the car in Köln. I mean, Ranken, that the Englishman you met on the train—there's reason to believe that he stole my car and then committed a murder."

Ranken put his hand on the wall to support himself. "Go in heaven!"

"They've given the case high priority. They believe the have the man's real name. It's Kenneth O'Rourke. He live in London. They've notified Interpol, and they're requestin the cooperation of Scotland Yard. It takes time, though. Mean while they want all the information they can get from you."

Ranken placed the telephone back on its stand. He couldn' bear to listen to any more. He leaned against the wall fo another few moments, then took a deep breath and returned to the living room.

His wife regarded him anxiously. "It's serious, isn't it?" she asked.

He nodded. He sank down in his chair and polished of the cognac in a gulp.

"Let me give you some more," his wife said.

He nodded again.

She refilled his glass.

But before he could drink the refill, the police arrived.

31

Cochran opened his eyes.

The bed was swaying, and there was a steady creaking. He didn't know where he was.

He groped for a light switch, but couldn't find one. His fingers encountered something cold. Suddenly he remembered that he was on a ship. The cold object was the faucet of a washbasin. He found the light switch and flicked it.

He'd fallen asleep with his clothes on. His suitcase was on the rack above his feet. His coat was hanging from a hook and was swinging slowly like the pendulum of a clock. He glanced at his watch. It showed a few minutes past three.

The motion was considerable. It was a rougher trip than most. He folded his arms under his head and crossed his ankles. He'd slept for more than three hours. That was unusual. He rarely slept on the way to Geneva. He'd trained himself not to.

After a while he sat up. Large beads of water were streaking across the outside of the porthole. Either it was raining or the waves were breaking hard against the hull. He noticed the newspaper on the floor beside his bunk. He'd read it on the train, but now, for lack of anything else to read, he went through it again. There had been a serious motor accident on the M-4—a man and his son killed, three others in hospital. A Member of Parliament was being sued for divorce on grounds of adultery. Blackpool was favored to win the football match against Burnley on Saturday. A German businessman had been kidnaped in a suburb of Buenos Aires.

The only article that he reread from beginning to end was the one about the Member of Parliament. There appeared to be a lot of bitterness on both sides, and his sympathies were aroused. Divorce had strange consequences. If it weren't for a divorce, he wouldn't be on this ship, reading the newspaper. Memories stirred. Nerves jerked. He tossed the newspaper aside and got to his feet. Normally on long crossings he remained locked in his cabin, but on this one there was no need for that.

The rolling of the ship made it difficult to walk. He had to hold on to the railing as he climbed the steps.

A number of people were asleep on the chairs and banquettes of the lounge. Evidently one woman had been seasick; she had a towel across her forehead. The lounge was quite still. He made his way back to the stairs and went up to the Boat Deck. Except for a stout old gentleman who was asleep in one of the chairs, the bar was deserted. Cochran noticed that an empty beer bottle was wedged between the man's leg and the arm of the chair, tucked there, apparently, to keep it from falling.

It was raining, all right. Raining hard. Nevertheless Cochran opened the door to the deck. The sky was pitch black. The rain was sweeping against the ship in gusts. He retreated into the corridor that led to the stairwell. And as he did so he caught a glimpse of a man in a brown suede topcoat ducking into the bar.

I'm not the only one who's restless, Cochran thought.

He returned to his cabin and lay down on his bunk. He didn't expect to fall asleep a second time. He did, though. He woke with a start when the stewardess entered the cabin a quarter to six.

"Coffee," she said, slapping the tray down beside the ashbasin.

He shaved, brushed his hair, put on his necktie and passed judgment on the reflection of himself in the mirror. It seemed to tell the truth: that he was a man who had slept in his clothes and whose sleep had been interrupted.

He carried his topcoat and suitcase up the stairs. The first-class dining room was filled with early risers who were finishing their breakfasts. He glanced at his watch. Twenty-five minutes past six. Still time for something to eat. He hesitated. Ordinarily he made it a point not to be one of the first passengers off the ship. He preferred to go through the passport-control and customs rooms when they were most crowded. But uneasiness was gnawing at him. The suitcase with the money— had it been placed on the ship? Had it been unloaded? Where was it?

He put on his topcoat, handed over his landing card and went down the gangplank. The rain that had lashed across the North Sea during the night was now lashing the coast of Holland. He turned up the collar of his coat and hurried across the quay to the terminal, wishing that he'd remembered to bring a hat or an umbrella. After all the years in London, he still hadn't learned. He was, he often thought, the only person in England who was never prepared for bad weather.

There were several dozen people waiting to go through passport control. Cochran took his place in what appeared to be the shortest of the lines, behind someone who was all parka and backpack. The line moved slowly. Cochran shoved his suitcase along with his foot. As they neared the passport-control officer's desk, the figure in front of Cochran turned,

and he got a brief look at the face. The hooded figure w
a woman. Then he began to tense. But unless the immigratio
service had been forewarned, there was nothing to fear fro
the passport-control officer.

The woman in the parka was cleared and, bent under th
weight of her backpack, she made her way into the custom
room. Cochran stepped up to the desk and presented h
passport.

The man in uniform studied him for what seemed an unrea
sonable length of time. "How long will you be in the Nethe
lands?" he asked.

"In transit," Cochran replied in a voice that sounded strang
to him. "En route to Switzerland."

The passport-control officer gave him another long loo
then stamped his passport.

Cochran took a deep breath, put the passport back in h
pocket and picked up his suitcase.

But his feeling of relief didn't last long.

The customs room had a U-shaped counter. The Port-
bag luggage was lined up in the center of the U, attende
by a porter with a trolley. There wasn't much of it—half
dozen suitcases and a few bulky parcels. Cochran's suitcas
was at one end of the line, separated from the rest, and directl
under a light. The green plastic seemed three shades lighte
than it had in his bedroom and glistened like water on
bright day. Two customs officers stood on the passenger:
side of the counter, and both of them were eyeing Cochran
suitcase with interest. They were talking to each other i
low voices. One of them nodded in the direction of the suitcas
and smiled.

Cochran watched. There was a steady stream of peopl
crossing the room from the passport-control desks to the ex
at the opposite end. Everyone was carrying at least one piec
of luggage, and a few were carrying more. The customs officer
were paying no attention to any of them; they appeared t

be concerned only with the luggage that had been checked.

Cochran's mind began to race. They've been tipped off, he thought. Not necessarily about me, but about someone. They're waiting for one particular item to be claimed.

He continued to eye them. They were young men, in their early twenties. The expressions on their faces weren't solemn. In fact, they appeared to be enjoying themselves. He began to think he was overreacting. They *hadn't* been tipped off. They weren't really concerned with his suitcase. They were just going through the motions of doing their job.

But presently a man detached himself from the procession that was moving toward the exit. He had a black vinyl suitcase in one hand and a British Airways flight bag slung over his shoulder. He went to the counter and, summoning the porter, gave him a claim check like the one Cochran had in his wallet. The porter picked one of the suitcases from the Port-a-bag line and placed it on the counter.

The customs officers immediately walked over to the man and spoke to him. He took a key from his pocket and began to open the suitcase.

Cochran left the customs room.

He paused in the corridor and tried to think what to do. He looked at his watch. Five minutes to seven. And the Rhein-gold left at seven seventeen. He had twenty-two minutes in which to figure something out.

On the spur of the moment, he could think of nothing.

He turned left and went to the Change. Normally on this run he didn't buy Dutch guilders; he bought Swiss francs. But now he bought guilders. Then he went across to the ticket office and scanned the schedule on the wall. It was a futile endeavor. No new trains had been added. There were the regular morning TEE's, the regular afternoon and early evening TEE's and the locals to Rotterdam that left every half-hour. No others. And the only direct train to Geneva was the Rheingold.

He walked out to the platform. The boat train to Amster dam was filling with passengers. The man who had been stopped by the customs officers was among them. Cochran saw him standing beside the train, waiting for the porter with the trolley to bring his luggage.

Rainwater was cascading from the roof of the platform. Cochran backed toward the terminal, thinking. He had the glimmering of an idea.

There were three alternatives. He could return to the customs room, claim his suitcase and hope for the best. But that would be ridiculous. Or he could wait for several hours to claim the suitcase, and take one of the locals to Rotterdam. From Rotterdam he could continue by a roundabout route. If he did that, he wouldn't arrive in Geneva when he'd said he would; he might not arrive until the next day. And he had no means of knowing how long he would have to hang around the Hook of Holland. The customs officers might be on duty for hours, or they might leave their post as soon as they were sure that all the passengers were off the ship—he couldn't be sure.

The third alternative was to locate a porter and let him claim the suitcase. Cochran had seen this done elsewhere. He didn't know whether it was possible at the Hook of Hol land, but he thought it was worth a try. If it worked, the porter would deliver the suitcase to him on the train before it pulled out. If it didn't—well, he'd simply have to wait for the right moment and go via Rotterdam.

Looking for a porter, he began to walk toward the platform where the Rheingold was waiting. He glanced at his watch. Five minutes past seven. He still had twelve minutes. He quickened his pace. The suitcase with his clothes bumped against his leg as he walked.

He came to the last of the terminal outbuildings and turned toward Platform 5B. The Rheingold was on the track where it always was, on the opposite side of the platform from the

hein Express. He peered down the platform. It was poorly
t, but a hundred yards ahead he could distinguish the shape
f a trolley.

It was going to be close. It could be done, though. Fortu-
ately, most of the passengers were already aboard the trains.
t would take the porter no more than five minutes to return
o the terminal and get the suitcase.

The porter came down the steps from one of the cars of
he Rheingold. The trolley appeared to be empty. Cochran
urried along the platform.

Suddenly someone spoke his name.

"Mr. Cochran?"

He halted. The voice had come from behind him. He turned
nd caught a glimpse of a man in a brown suede coat. He
ad an inkling that he'd seen the coat before.

"Yes," he said. And an instant later he felt a blinding pain
t the back of his head.

His hand opened. The suitcase fell to the platform. His
knees began to buckle.

He felt another blinding pain.

Everything went black.

32

There was an unpleasant odor. And he was freezing.

He looked down at himself. He was practically naked. His trousers and underpants were down around his ankles. His shirt, tie, jacket and topcoat were in a heap on the floor.

He was shivering. He hugged himself, but it didn't help. He reached for his topcoat and missed. But the movement set off a violent throbbing in his head. Still clutching his shoulder with one hand, he touched the back of his head with the other and felt a lump. He must have fainted and hit his head on something. Yet he was sitting. Sitting on a toilet seat, in fact. Was it possible to faint and not fall?

The shivering grew worse. His teeth began to chatter. He had to put some clothes on. The cold was too much for him. He made another pass at his coat. Again he missed. He managed to clasp two fingers around the collar of his shirt, however, and pull it toward him. The effort of putting the shirt on was too strenuous. All he could do was wrap the cloth around mself and hold the ends close to his chest.

Yes, he was definitely in one of the booths of a public
ashroom. But where? And why? He had no recollection of
etting sick.

He listened. Wind and rain. That seemed right. It had
een raining. It had been raining on the ship. It had been
ining. . . . Suddenly he remembered. He was in Holland.

The throbbing in his head continued. And there was some-
ing wrong with his right hand too. It was sore. He examined
and saw a tiny red mark over one of the veins. Also a
w spots of dried blood. He frowned.

Rain, wind, Holland . . . A suitcase. There was something
out a suitcase. Something about customs . . . He had to
t dressed. He couldn't remain as he was, naked and shivering
one of the booths of a public washroom in the Hook of
olland.

The *Hook* of Holland?

Of course. The terminal at the Hook of Holland. A suitcase
led with money. The money belonged to a . . . He couldn't
emember the man's name. He could remember what the
an looked like, though. They'd met in the buffet at the
ictoria Air Terminal.

The first thing was to get dressed. He couldn't imagine
hy he'd taken off his shirt and tie. He'd better put them
n again, however, before he froze to death. His suit jacket,
o. And his topcoat. He'd been cold before, but he'd never
een this cold. Some hot coffee was what he needed. Several
ups of hot coffee. Something to raise his body temperature.
here was a place to eat in the terminal. He was sure of
hat. He couldn't remember where it was, but he knew he'd
ad a meal there once.

His hands were shaking so violently that it took him several
inutes to get his arms through the sleeves of the shirt and
fasten the buttons. Then, cautiously, he stood up. The
rembling was as bad as it had been before, but he found

that he didn't feel particularly weak. He simply felt tired.
Except for the trembling, which he couldn't control, there
didn't seem to be anything wrong with him. A headache,
that was all. And the headache had been caused by his striking
his head against something. But when he bent down to put
up his shorts and his trousers, the headache became considerably worse. He had to lean against the wall to tuck in his
shirt and zip up his fly. He dreaded having to bend again
to get his jacket and topcoat. He did it, however.

There was a long slash in the lining of both the suit jacket
and the topcoat. That was odd. The slashes looked as if they'd
been made with a sharp object of some sort.

It didn't make sense.

The trembling began to subside. Looking at his coats, he
had a sudden urge to cry. There was nothing to cry about,
though. He was in Holland, he'd got sick, he'd hit his head,
his clothes were torn. Why did he want to cry?

He put on the jacket and coat and stuffed his necktie into
a pocket. Then he left the booth. There was no one else in
the washroom. It appeared to be a place that was seldom
used.

He opened the door to the outside. There were no trains
beside the platform. Rain was blowing across it from the exposed sides. And he was evidently at the very end—he could
barely see the lights of the terminal building in the distance.

It came to him that he'd been on his way to Geneva and
that he'd missed his train.

Geneva. The man's name was Evans. That was it. Peter
Evans. He was the client of a lawyer named Michael Garwood.

Memories began to rush at him. Evans, Garwood, the
money . . . His vest was gone. That was what had happened.
Someone had stolen the vest with the money.

No, that *wasn't* what had happened. He hadn't been wearing the vest. The money was in a suitcase.

He recalled the customs room, the shiny green vinyl. He had to claim the suitcase. He had to get the money.

But someone might have *tried* to steal the vest.

That was it. Someone had tried to steal the vest. Who, though?

He walked along the wet platform toward the terminal. He remembered getting off the ship, going through passport control. He remembered being afraid to claim the suitcase. What had happened then?

His memory failed him. He knew he had to claim the suitcase, however.

He quickened his pace. The throbbing in his head accelerated too. Could someone have hit him over the head?

But who had known?

He reached the outbuilding that housed the stationmaster's office. He passed a bicycle rack. He entered the terminal through the main entrance. To his right was the Change. One attendant was on duty. To his left was the ticket office. One attendant was on duty there too. He peered into the customs room. The porter was sitting on the counter, scratching his neck. All of the baggage had been claimed except one piece: Cochran's.

There was only a single customs officer present now.

Cochran hesitated, then retreated into the corridor. A sign pointed to the buffet. He followed the arrow.

The other customs officer was having breakfast. He was sitting at a table with some of the passport-control officers.

Cochran went to the counter, ordered a cup of black coffee, paid for it and took it to a table. Again he had a strange urge to cry.

He tried to reconstruct the events leading to his regaining consciousness in the washroom. He touched the lump on his head. He looked at his hand. The red mark could have been made by a needle. The uncontrollable trembling, the urge to cry—could those be the aftereffects of a drug?

He swallowed a mouthful of hot coffee. It burned his throa but he began to feel better.

He concentrated on the suitcase in the customs roor Sooner or later he had to get it. But he'd had another suitca with him. What had happened to the other suitcase?

It didn't matter. Nothing was in it but clothes. He'd ha it in his hand, though.

Had someone spoken his name? He had a vague recollectic that someone had.

He reached into his back pocket. His wallet was still ther He took it out and opened it. His British and Dutch mone was intact. So was the claim check. Whoever had tried t rob him had been after only one thing: the vest.

But then a new thought came to him. Whoever had trie to rob him had been disappointed. It was possible that th person was still lurking somewhere in the terminal, waitin for him to make a move.

Cochran looked nervously around the room. There wer no tourists. Only government employees.

Someone might be outside, however.

He finished his coffee and went back to the counter for second cup. As he was paying for it, he saw the other custom officer come through the doorway and join his co-worker.

Cochran deposited the second cup of coffee on the tabl he'd been sitting at and left the buffet.

The porter was alone in the customs room.

Cochran went up to the counter. "Missed my train," h said with a smile.

The porter gave him a blank look. It was obvious that h didn't understand English.

Cochran presented the claim check, and the porter, wit an air of complete indifference, gave him the suitcase. Cochrar quickly carried it out to the platform.

The platform was deserted. But fifty yards beyond it, or

he other side of the parking lot, he saw a small train taking
on passengers. The local to Rotterdam, he thought. He began
to run.

It was almost noon when the train from Rotterdam arrived
at Amsterdam's Central Station.

Cochran carried the suitcase down the steps to the underpass and through the underpass into the main concourse.

The storage lockers were at the end of the building, near
the checkroom. He found an empty one and noted the time
limit: seventy-two hours. Then he peeled the shipping label
from the suitcase and shoved the suitcase in, deposited a coin
and pocketed the key.

It was still raining. There was a long line at the taxi rank.
He took his place at the end of the line and waited.

After twenty minutes his turn came. He opened the door
and climbed into the taxi's back seat.

"Reijnier Vinkeles Kade," he told the driver.

33

The Audi was exactly where he'd left it.

The motor started without difficulty.

But the drive took longer than O'Rourke had expected. The rain made it difficult to read the road signs. The pavement was slippery. And despite the early hour, traffic was heavy. The E-36, which had been uncrowded when he'd traveled along it before, was almost bumper to bumper with commuters driving into Rotterdam, and because there were only two lanes it was impossible to pass. The blades of the windshield wipers clicked in an irritating rhythm; the sky was totally black; the stream of taillights ahead of him stretched as far as he could see. The glow from the headlights of the creeping procession of cars illuminated nothing but greenhouses. The soil of Holland didn't produce plants; it produced greenhouses. There were miles and miles of them.

After Maasdijk, conditions improved. The E-36 became wider. But five kilometers beyond Schiedam, where the

E-36 crossed the E-10, O'Rourke missed the turn. He realized his mistake immediately, but it took him twenty minutes to correct it. And when at last he was on the E-10, heading in the right direction, he found that he was less confident than he usually was while driving. He had no map—he didn't need one; the route had been firmly fixed in his mind for a week. He knew precisely which cities he'd pass. Delft, Den Haag and Leiden, then into Amsterdam from the southwest. Since he hadn't known what Garwood's plans would be, he'd even worked out alternative routes. The only thing he hadn't worked out was an escape route. He hadn't thought he'd need one. Garwood would pay him the balance of the three thousand, he'd take the first plane back to London and that would be that. He hadn't considered that he might be tricked.

But that was what had happened. Someone had tricked him.

At the outskirts of Den Haag he hesitated. There was an interchange. If he went straight ahead, he'd wind up in Amsterdam; if he turned east, in Gouda. From Gouda he could head south, back to Rotterdam and through Rotterdam to the Belgian border. He was tempted. Garwood wouldn't know where he'd gone, and from Belgium he could get to England. He'd be in England by mid-afternoon. If the planes were flying. With the bloody rain and poor visibility, they might not be. Besides, what would he do once he was in England? Garwood would eventually catch up with him.

He went straight ahead.

It was all Trumper's fault. Trumper had got him into it. And now he'd been tricked.

The questions were, by whom and for what reason?

He intended to find out. He also intended to collect the fifteen hundred. The extra four hundred too. It wasn't his fault that he'd ruined a good suit and shirt.

At Leiden there was another interchange. Utrecht lay to the east. From Utrecht he could continue on to Germany.

But the same problem presented itself: Garwood would catch up with him in England, and then what? Garwood would never believe that he hadn't stolen the money, that there hadn't been any money to steal.

Garwood wouldn't believe him anyway, perhaps. But at least he had the suitcase. The suitcase was evidence of a sort.

Was Garwood the one who had tricked him? Probably not. Most likely, Garwood had been misled by the informer. Deliberately. The scene in the air terminal had been staged as part of a scheme. The money was still in England or was already in Switzerland. There was certainly more to the scheme than Garwood knew about. Garwood wasn't as bright as he thought himself.

Gradually the sky turned lighter. And as the morning advanced, traffic on the E-10 became even heavier. Half of Holland, it seemed to O'Rourke, commuted to Rotterdam; the other half, to Amsterdam. Furthermore, the Dutch were the worst drivers he'd ever encountered. Even in the rain they traveled at ridiculously high speeds, cutting back and forth from one lane to another.

The informer had the money. Of that O'Rourke was almost certain. Would Garwood believe it, though?

Biting his lips, peering intently through the windshield, gripping the wheel with a firmness that was abnormal for him, O'Rourke reflected.

It had been so easy. The American had given him no trouble at all. One of the baggage porters had stared at them, but had said nothing. Some of the passengers might have seen them, too, from the windows of the train. But O'Rourke was positive that to an observer it had appeared that a man was helping his sick friend. There had been no resistance to the needle. The search had taken less than two minutes. He'd had time to go back for the suitcase, to carry it to the car, to examine it. The suitcase hadn't even been locked. Everything had gone exactly according to plan.

Except that the American hadn't been carrying the money.

A sign with a picture of an airplane on it indicated that e was approaching Schiphol Airport.

He wouldn't have to go to Germany or Belgium. He could ave for England directly from here. He would be in England efore noon.

He slowed the car. The temptation was very strong.

When he reached the exit to the airport, the temptation ot the better of him. He turned.

Leaving the car in a parking stall, he entered the vast termi- al building.

The KLM flight to London had been canceled.

British Airways simply didn't know. The flight to London vas a turnaround flight, and the plane hadn't even left Heath- ow yet. Considering the weather, there was a possibility that t wouldn't. More information was expected shortly.

O'Rourke left the terminal, went back to the car for Cochran's suitcase, then found a taxi. "Hilton Hotel," he napped.

The doorman tried to take the suitcase, but O'Rourke told im to keep his bloody hands to himself.

Garwood was sitting in the center of the lobby near the ooded fireplace. He raised a finger to attract O'Rourke's ttention, but O'Rourke had already seen him and was on he way over, scowling.

Garwood looked at the suitcase. "What's that?"

"Evidence."

Garwood began to scowl also. "Of what?"

"Of your making a fool of me."

All that moved were Garwood's eyes. He glanced quickly to the left and right. The fireplace was the focal point of the room. Half a dozen people were within hearing distance.

"You tricked me," O'Rourke said. His eyes were flashing with anger.

"Shut up," Garwood said. "Come with me."

They crossed the lobby to the elevators, Garwood in the lead. A porter ran over to them and tried to take the suitcase, as the doorman had done. "Bugger off," O'Rourke said sharply.

They rode up to the fifth floor and walked along the corridor. Garwood unlocked the door to his room. O'Rourke put the suitcase on the unmade bed and opened it. He threw the contents into the air and let them fall to the floor. "There's your vest," he said. "There's your money. You've made a fool of me."

Garwood's eyes narrowed. "Explain," he said. His voice was low. His face was the color of chalk dust. "At once."

" 'Explain,' " O'Rourke mimicked. " 'Explain.' *You're* the one who'd better explain, Mr. Bloody Solicitor. I don't like to be made a fool of. I don't like being sent on a wild-goose chase. I expect my nineteen hundred pounds, and I swear if you try to cheat me you'll go right through that window."

"O'Rourke, I'm warning you."

" 'O'Rourke, I'm warning you.' I like that. That's very clever. I'm telling you, Mr. Solicitor, Mr. High and Mighty Garwood, if you try to cheat me, you'll go right through that window. Any explaining that's going to be done here is going to be done by you. Because there was no money. No vest, no money, nothing. Do you understand that? Nothing!" He picked up the suitcase and threw it against the headboard of the bed. A picture fell to the floor. "You tricked me!" he shouted. "You made a fool of me!"

"Shut up, O'Rourke. Tell me where the money is. I warned you—"

" 'Tell me where the money is.' " O'Rourke advanced on Garwood. Garwood retreated. O'Rourke grabbed his forearm and squeezed. Garwood's face went a shade paler. "You tell *me* where the money is," O'Rourke said. "Because there *was* no sodding money. There *was* no sodding vest. There was nothing but a suitcase full of clothes. What do you say to hat, Mr. Solicitor? A suitcase full of clothes!"

"Release my arm, O'Rourke."

"A suitcase full of clothes!" O'Rourke shouted. But he released Garwood's arm.

"You followed the wrong man," Garwood said in a strangled voice.

" 'You followed the wrong man.' That's rich, that is. I followed the *right* man. I followed the man you told me to follow. I followed him to the Victoria Air Terminal. I saw the man he met. I saw him give the other man a receipt for a suitcase and I saw the other man claim it at the left-luggage room. I followed the other man home. Would you like to know where he lives? Would you like a description of him? I'll tell you where he lives. I'll give you a description of him." He proceeded to do so.

Garwood walked over the clothes on the floor and sat down on the bed, frowning and rubbing the arm O'Rourke had seized. "That's Cochran," he admitted.

"So don't tell *me* I followed the wrong man," O'Rourke went on. "I followed the *right* man. I didn't only follow him to bloody Holland, I followed him before he ever left England. I stood outside his house yesterday from two thirty in the afternoon until he left to get on the sodding train. In the cold I stood there for three and a half hours, till I was half froze. I got on the train with him. I got on the boat with him. I got off the boat with him. I did everything I said I was going to do. But he wasn't wearing any vest under his shirt and he wasn't carrying any load of money."

Abstractedly, Garwood continued to rub his arm. He stared at the clothes on the floor. "It's impossible," he said.

"It's not impossible. It's possible as anything ever. It's the informer. The man I followed to the air terminal. There was no money in that suitcase at the left-luggage room. There never had been. It was all a trick."

Garwood shook his head.

"Cochran didn't *have* the money."

"Cochran *did* have the money." Garwood looked up. "Tell me what happened. Exactly what happened. Step by step."

O'Rourke eyed him. He believes me, he thought. He began to relax. And to relate the events of the past twenty hours.

Garwood eyed him in return. Psychopathic he may be, he thought, but he didn't steal the money. He's telling the truth. He listened in silence until O'Rourke had finished his account, then stared again at the clothes on the floor. "Go back to the customs room," he said at last. "You said he stopped there for some little time."

"That's right. He stopped there for almost five minutes. I watched him from the door. It was, you might say, like he was studying what was going on. For future operations, I thought. Keeping up to date, if you take my meaning."

"Then he simply left?"

O'Rourke nodded. "Went to that bank, like, that they have there. Exchanged some money. Then he went into the room where they sell the tickets, but he didn't buy a ticket—it was more like he was passing the time—then he went out to the train that was at the first platform, the train to Amsterdam. He stood there maybe a minute or so, then he went to get on the Geneva train, the Rheingold. There was no one else about—it was like the first time I was there, last week—and I—"

"Did he appear to be nervous?"

"Not really."

"And this suitcase—the one you brought here—he had that with him all the while?"

O'Rourke nodded.

"Odd," Garwood mused.

O'Rourke smiled. He was beginning to feel vindicated. "Odd?"

"Why did he stand there in the customs room? What was

e doing? Could he have been waiting to claim a suitcase? ou say he wasn't nervous, but you couldn't really know. Ie might have had another suitcase. He might have checked t in London. There is such a service, I believe. Or given it o one of the porters on the ship."

"With the *money* in it?"

"Possibly. What other reason could he have had for remaining in the customs room, the last place one would expect le'd want to linger?"

O'Rourke recalled the period when Cochran had been out of sight at Liverpool Street Station. He'd omitted that period rom the account he'd given Garwood. It was conceivable hat during that period Cochran had checked a suitcase or exchanged one with a confederate. On the other hand, Cochran had been eating. And O'Rourke was quite certain hat Cochran had had only one suitcase with him when he'd eft the building on Basil Street and that it was the suitcase which was now in this room.

Garwood pursed his thin lips. "Is there any way he might have got on that train?" he asked presently.

O'Rourke shook his head. "None. That I *know.*"

"Then it's safe to assume he's still in Holland. And I'm nclined to believe that the money is too. Yes, almost certainly. Somewhere here in Holland. Definitely."

"I doubt it," O'Rourke said. "The money, I mean. I don't think he had it. I think he was a decoy, like."

Garwood ignored him. "He wouldn't get on a plane with it. He'd have to take a train. There are no afternoon trains to Geneva. At least, I don't *think* there are." He got up and began to pace the floor. "He might go to Rotterdam. The logical place is here, though: Amsterdam. What condition was he in?"

"You could have cut him open and taken out his appendix and he wouldn't have known. I probably should have."

"No, you did right. Quite right."

"What about my money?"

"When I have my money, my client's money, you'll get yours. Not before."

O'Rourke took the weapon from his pocket. The shape of the wrench was plainly visible through the sock. Humming he began to tap the weapon against the palm of his left hand.

Garwood gave him a cold look. "Put that thing away, O'Rourke. I'm the only hope you have of getting safely out of this country and back to England. Just you remember that."

"Is that so?"

"Yes, that is so. Now leave me alone. I have some thinking to do."

"Leave you alone? Where am I supposed to go?"

"Get yourself a room somewhere. Get yourself a room here. The hotel isn't crowded. Everyone is home for the holidays. Your job isn't over. When it *is* over, you'll get paid."

O'Rourke considered. Finally he put the wrench back in his pocket. "What are you going to do?" he asked.

"Contact my client," Garwood replied. "But not for several hours. Now leave me. Get yourself a room and stay in it. I'll be in touch with you."

O'Rourke considered further. The planes were grounded. And he had no intention of leaving without the balance of the money.

Treasonous thoughts again entered his mind. They seemed less treasonous than they had before.

"Right," he said cheerfully. "This isn't a bad hotel. I'll get myself a room."

34

The look of joy on Ruth's face changed almost immediately to one of alarm. "You're not well!" she exclaimed.

Cochran gave her a crooked smile. "I had a slight accident."

"Come," said Beatrix Coertsen, taking his arm. "Sit down."

He let himself be led to a velvet-upholstered chair with crocheted antimacassars on the arms, and dropped into it. Both women stood in front of him, regarding him with anxious eyes.

"Ruth," he said, and reached for her hand. He hadn't been able to anticipate what the sight of her would do to him. He'd thought that it might in some strange way cause him to weaken, and now he found that it did. He had the sudden feeling that nothing really mattered, nothing beyond the four walls of the room.

"Your hand is like ice!" Ruth cried. She turned to Beatrix. "Do we have some brandy?"

"Of course." The Dutch woman went to a tall cabinet and opened it.

"Never mind," Cochran said. "I'm all right."

"You're *not* all right," Ruth insisted.

He pulled her toward him and patted the arm of the chair. "Sit here. Let me look at you."

She obeyed. Then she saw the back of his head. "My God, darling, you have a lump the size of an egg! What happened?"

He'd promised himself that he wouldn't lie. They were entitled to the truth, both of them. But at the moment the truth was more than he could manage. He needed a little time. "I had an encounter," he said.

"Where? With whom? You're pale as a ghost. You ought to lie down."

Beatrix brought a bottle and a glass. "Ruth," she said sharply, "calm yourself. Here," she said to Cochran, "if you wish a drink, it is on the table."

"Thank you," he said. She didn't look like one of the world's leading authorities on the Franco-Prussian War, he thought. She looked like his grandmother. He half expected her to tell him to hang up his clothes and then do his homework.

"But he's had an accident," Ruth protested. "Look at this lump on the back of his head."

"So?" said Beatrix. "He had an encounter." She smiled at him.

He decided that he liked her.

"This is an unexpected pleasure," she said. "Ruth has been telling me about you."

He didn't doubt it. He couldn't think of a reply. "Your English is excellent," he said politely.

"So is my French, my German and my Italian," she said. "It is my Dutch that sometimes earns me criticism. Perhaps you would like some tea?"

He nodded. The motion made his headache worse. "Please."

She left the room.

Cochran yawned.

"You really ought to lie down," Ruth said. "You might have a concussion."

"I probably do," he said. "But I've got this far with it, so I guess it's nothing to worry about."

"You were on your way to Switzerland, is that it?"

He'd promised himself that he wouldn't lie about that either. "Yes."

She sighed and withdrew her hand from his.

Beatrix returned. "The tea will be ready soon."

"John was on his way to Switzerland," Ruth told her.

He gathered that they'd discussed him at length and that Beatrix understood the implication.

She ignored it, however. "You really ought to take off your coat," she said to Cochran.

He'd forgotten that he still had it on. Half rising, he struggled out of it. And was immediately sorry. For both women's eyes widened when they saw the long rip in the lining.

He put the coat on the table, beside the bottle of brandy, and sank back into the chair. Truth time. "O.K.," he said. "Somebody tried to rob me. That's why I'm here."

Neither woman spoke.

"My suit coat is torn like that too," he added.

Beatrix was the first to recover. "*Tried* to rob you?"

"Right. He didn't succeed."

"Of what?"

"Of some money I was carrying. It happened at the terminal at the Hook of Holland."

"When?" Ruth asked.

"Early this morning."

There was another silence.

"The police have not been told, I assume," Beatrix said presently.

Indeed they had discussed him, he thought. And the Dutch woman's mind was swift. "There was no need to tell them anything," he said. "The attempt failed. All I lost was the suitcase with my clothes. But I needed a place to . . . regroup."

"You have no hotel room?" she asked.

He shook his head. It was as painful as nodding.

"So the money is . . . where?"

"In a safe place."

Ruth got up and went to the window. She stood there, with her back to them. She was obviously upset. Her shoulders were rising and falling as if she were doing breathing exercises. He wanted to go over to her, but thought better of it.

From the next room came the whistle of a teakettle. Beatrix left to give the kettle her attention.

Cochran watched Ruth. Finally he could stand it no longer. He went to where she was standing and put his arms around her. She didn't respond.

"I've missed you," he said.

"Rain and fog," she said. "You can hardly see the Hilton."

He looked. He'd recognized the hotel when he'd got out of the taxi. It was less than two hundred yards away, across the canal and to the right of the bridge. But the weather was even worse now. In addition to the steady rain, there was a fog that was getting denser by the minute. The hotel was a ghostly shape that was alternately visible and invisible.

"I've missed you," he repeated.

"You're using us," she said.

He dropped his arms.

"You came here because you had no place else to go."

He said nothing.

"I wrote Todd. I know you didn't want me to, but I did it anyway."

The feeling he'd had earlier, of wanting to cry, returned. He fought it. "There's no future for us. I told you that. You didn't believe me."

She turned and put her head on his shoulder. She began to breathe hard again. He stroked her hair.

"Is it serious?" she asked at last.

"No."

She gave him a questioning look.

"It's not serious," he said. "It might have been, but it's not."

"Come," said Beatrix. "Have some tea."

Cochran glanced over his shoulder. Beatrix was standing in the doorway, with one hand on a teacart. He led Ruth back to where they'd been sitting, and Beatrix pushed the cart over to them. On it was a Delft tea service and an apple cake. She began to fill the cups.

For the first time Cochran took in the details of the room. The white lace curtains and the gleaming copper bowls with plants in them; the wall of bookshelves with books piled on top of other books; the tall cabinet that appeared to be at least a hundred years old; the china bric-a-brac. It was, he thought, the homiest, most comfortable room he'd ever been in. It made him long for something he'd never had: genuine stability.

"Thank you," he said, accepting a cup of tea and a plate with a large piece of apple cake on it. "And just in case you're wondering, the police in Holland are not looking for me."

Ruth flushed.

"Drink your tea," Beatrix said. "You really are quite pale."

He put the plate with the cake on the table in front of him. "I've thrust myself on you," he said, "and you're entitled to know. I was carrying a large amount of money from London to Geneva. It wasn't my money. I was being paid a fee to carry it. As far as England is concerned, I was violating a law. As far as Switzerland is concerned, I wasn't. As for Holland—Holland wasn't involved; I was merely passing through. But evidently someone found out I had the money and tried to steal it. I don't know who, or how he found out, or whether it was one man operating on his own or a group of men. At any rate, this morning as I was about to get on the train at the Hook of Holland I was, well, assaulted. I didn't have the money on me, so the thief or thieves didn't get it. But I had to change my plans." He drank some of the tea.

"Is that what you do for a living?" Ruth asked. "Carry money?"

"It's called smuggling," he replied. "Yes, that's what I do for a living." He drank some more tea. "Now you know."

"A very old profession," Beatrix observed.

"Like prostitution," he agreed.

She smiled. "In Holland prostitution is legal." Her smile faded. "What will you do?"

He put the cup and saucer on the table and picked up the plate with the cake. But then he put it down again. He wasn't hungry. What he was was sleepy. Very sleepy. "Call the man I'm supposed to deliver the money to. Tell him what happened. Tell him to come here and pick it up. He won't have any trouble getting it from here to Geneva. The hard part is getting it from London here."

"Suppose he refuses," Ruth said.

"He can't refuse. He wants it."

Once more the Dutch woman demonstrated the swiftness of her mind. "You need an apartment in which to stay. You wouldn't be safe in a hotel."

He started to nod, but remembered that nodding hurt. "True. I don't want to stay with you, though. I don't believe I was followed here this morning—I'm almost sure I wasn't—but—" He yawned.

"You should lie down," Ruth said. "I really do think you have a concussion."

"I'm lucky I don't have a fractured skull. But that wasn't what I was going to say. I was going to say you may not be safe either. Someone may have been following me for some

ime. In that case, he may have seen you. He may know
where you are. He—"

"I think it most improbable," said Beatrix, "but it is good
of you to warn us. . . . Eat some cake. And put more sugar
in your tea. You should have sugar. Then, Ruth is right—
you should lie down."

"If I could use the telephone . . ."

"Of course. Come with me."

The telephone was on a table in a narrow hall between
the two bedrooms. Beatrix helped him place the call. She
waited until the switchboard operator at the Hôtel Richemond
answered, then turned the telephone over to Cochran and
went back to the living room.

"Peter Evans," he said. Be there, he thought as he listened
to the double buzzes at the other end of the line.

Evans answered. "Yes?" He sounded as if the ringing of
the telephone had given him a scare.

"Evans? Cochran here. I've run into a problem."

"Cochran? A problem? Er—where are you? What's
happened?"

"You must have talked. Someone tried to steal the money."

"Talked? Steal the money? Oh, my God!"

"It's all right. The money's safe. But you're going to have
to come to Amsterdam to get it."

"Amsterdam? But I can't. I mean, we agreed . . . I didn't
talk. I didn't tell a soul. Why Amsterdam? I—I—"

"Look, you want the money, you have to come here. That's
all there is to it. Be here by tomorrow. They have banks
here. They have safe-deposit boxes. You can—"

"But we agreed. I mean, I'm paying you. I swear I didn't
mention a thing to anyone. I—I— Who was it? Are you
sure the money's all right? I—" He paused for breath. There
was real panic in his voice. "I—I can't come to Amsterdam.
I mean, it's snowing here. We're having a snowstorm. I'm
sure there are no planes. I—"

"Take a train. There's a night train from Basel. I took last winter. It'll get you here tomorrow morning. I'll mee you at the Centraal Station. I'll meet you tomorrow at—at— Give the man time, he thought. "At noon."

"But—but—Cochran, I— The Centraal Station? I don' know. I— How will I find you?"

"Look for me. I'll be there somewhere. Noon tomorrow After that I'm going back to England and you can whistl for your money. And keep your damn mouth shut. Don' talk to anyone. Understand?"

"But—but—"

Cochran hung up. He stood by the telephone for a moment annoyed by the feeling that he should have been even mor emphatic. Then he yawned. He'd made his point, he decided

He returned to the living room.

"I put more sugar in your tea," Ruth said. There was pro found anxiety in her eyes.

He forced himself to smile. "Everything's all right." He sat down again in the deep chair and drank some tea. He was beginning to feel warmer. But the tiredness was getting worse. It was almost more than he could cope with. "Don' look so worried."

"Close your eyes for a few minutes," Beatrix suggested to him.

He resisted. This was no time to close his eyes. He had to find a place to stay. He couldn't endanger the two women Yet . . .

His need overcame his will. His eyes closed as if of their own accord. And seconds later he was sound asleep.

35

The two stone lions were blanketed with snow. So was the statue of Charles II on horseback. Shrubs, trees, the fountain—everything in the Square de Mont-Blanc had a thick white coating. And yet the snow continued to fall. Driven by the wind, it was a swirling curtain that obscured everything. The city seemed to have vanished. Evans could scarcely see across the little square to the Hôtel de la Paix.

Turning away from the window, he resumed his pacing. The concierge had assured him that there were no planes leaving Cointrin Airport and had been quite rude when asked how long this situation might prevail—he wasn't a weather forecaster, he'd said. The Holland-Italy Express left Basel for Amsterdam shortly before midnight. If the gentleman wished to connect with it, he should take the train from Geneva at 18:24. Even the trains were liable to be delayed in such weather.

Fool, Evans thought for the twentieth time. You didn't

even ask Cochran where he could be reached. You stuttere
and stammered and learned nothing at all. It's the same faul
you've always had: strong personalities make you ineffectua
You're too easily put on the defensive, and when you're o
the defensive you become slow-witted.

He interrupted his pacing and his self-criticism to ope
the window. The room was much too warm. There appeare
to be no means of adjusting the heat. Yet when he opene
the window, the room became too cold. He'd been up mos
of the night, trying to control the temperature.

Had Cochran been telling the truth? He'd seemed a depend
able sort. Yet he was a professional criminal.

What does he stand to gain by making me come to Amster
dam? Who knows what a man like that might have in th
back of his mind?

Once more Evans picked up the telephone. It was the thir
time in less than an hour that he'd tried to reach Michae
Garwood. The previous two times, he'd been told that Mr
Garwood hadn't come in and hadn't telephoned to repor
his whereabouts. And there had been no answer at his flat
either.

No, he heard the switchboard operator in London tell the
overseas operator, Mr. Garwood hadn't yet arrived.

He hung up, sat down on the bed and put his head in
his hands. He simply didn't know what to do. Cochran had
seemed so confident, back in London, that he'd allowed himself to feel confident too. And now . . .

He had to do *some*thing. But what? Suppose that he went
to Amsterdam and walked into a trap. Suppose, on the other
hand, that he *didn't* go to Amsterdam and Cochran carried
out his threat.

He ran a hand through his hair. The whole thing was a mistake. He'd been wrong to let Uncle Michael persuade him.
Now he might lose everything. A man like Cochran . . .

The room was definitely too cold. He really ought to close

he window. He couldn't bring himself to get off the bed, however.

He was no match for a man like Cochran. He'd realized that, the first time they'd met. Cochran was a hardened—

The sound of the telephone made him jump.

Cochran, he thought wildly as he grabbed the instrument from its base. Cochran ringing back.

"Peter?"

"Uncle Michael!" Evans almost dissolved with relief. "I'm so glad you called. I—I'm in a frightful predicament. Cochran rang me an hour ago. Something's gone wrong, he said. Someone tried to steal the money. He wants me to come to Amsterdam. He *insists* I come to Amsterdam. He—"

"Amsterdam? Why Amsterdam? What did you tell him, Peter? What did he tell you? I don't like the sound of this."

"I didn't tell him anything. I—I didn't know what to tell him. He—he didn't give me—he didn't give me a chance. He simply told me to be at the Centraal Station in Amsterdam at noon tomorrow. If I wasn't there, he said—"

"Peter, I warned you. I told you the sort of man he is. Unfortunately, he was the only man available, but that doesn't make him trustworthy. You knew that. You knew that he's entirely dependent on this man Arlen. He'd like to get free of him, but he can't. Now, with all this money in his hands that Arlen knows nothing about . . . I don't like the sound of this at all, Peter. You're not equipped to deal with a man of his sort."

"I know that, but I—"

"You'd best let me deal with him. Tomorrow at noon, you say? What part of the station?"

"He didn't say. He simply said—he said I should look for him. He—"

"Very clever of him. Well, you stay right where you are. I'll meet him at the station. I'm accustomed to dealing with men who feel they're above the law. Furthermore, I have a

hold over him. Don't worry. You'll get your money. You'll
have it by tomorrow night, if I have to bring it to you myself
I'll fly to Amsterdam immediately."

"But you can't, Uncle Michael. It—it's snowing."

"Snowing?"

"The airport is closed."

"Use your head, Peter. It's not snowing here, it's raining
You're in Geneva, man. I'm not."

"Ah. I—I'm afraid I'm so upset I—"

"I understand. But you can stop fretting. Give yourself a
good dinner and a good night's sleep. I'll ring you tomorrow
from Amsterdam."

"But—"

"No buts, Peter. I feel responsible. I got you into this
You just relax. I'll handle Cochran. It's fortunate that I
telephoned."

"I know. I—"

"Goodbye, Peter. These calls are expensive."

Evans was about to agree when he heard the click that
meant Garwood had hung up.

He put the telephone back on its base and went to close
the window.

The snow was coming down harder than ever.

Again he hadn't had a chance to say everything that was
on his mind.

He began to think.

After a few minutes he went to the telephone.

"I'd like to place a trunk call to London," he told the
operator, and gave her the number of Garwood's office. "I'll
speak with anyone," he added.

As before, the operator told him she'd ring him when the
call was completed. As before, he said he'd remain on the
line. As before, the call went through very quickly.

He recognized the voice of the switchboard operator in
Garwood's office, and she recognized his.

"Mr. Garwood hasn't been in all day, I'm afraid, Mr. Evans. 's unusual, but I'm afraid I can't tell you where he can be :ached."

"Tell me," Evans said, "what's the weather in London this :ternoon?"

"Quite chilly, actually. Not nearly as nice as yesterday. I'm 'earing a wool sweater over my blouse, and even with that—"

"Is it raining?"

"No, it's simply cold. As I said—"

"Has it rained at all today?"

"No. It's dry enough. But I should have worn—"

"Thank you," Evans said. "Thank you very much."

He did some more thinking. Then he placed a call to the wissair office. All flights from Geneva to Amsterdam were anceled, he was told.

"What about from elsewhere?" he asked. "I mean, if I— r—took the train to—er—Zürich, and then, say, to Frankfurt. mean, can I get to Amsterdam by plane from anywhere?"

The Swissair clerk told him she didn't know whether he ould or not.

He placed a call to Amsterdam's Schiphol Airport. And earned that the airport had been closed all day due to rain nd fog.

He realized then that he'd been more of a fool than he'd imagined.

His watch showed twenty minutes to three. The train to 3asel didn't leave for nearly four hours. But possibly there vas an earlier train, he thought as he began to pack.

36

"I must have dozed off," Cochran said.

Ruth smiled, and put her book aside. "You slept for over three hours."

"I don't believe it."

"It's almost five o'clock."

"My God!" He tried to get out of the chair, but couldn't. Someone had covered him with an afghan, and his feet were tangled in it. He untangled them. "I've got to get out of here!"

"Relax," Ruth said. "Beatrix should be back any minute."

He stood up. "Where's my coat?"

"In the closet. I sewed the lining. But you can't go out. Until Beatrix gets back, there's no place for you to go. And it's still pouring."

"Where'd she go?"

"To see a friend of hers about giving you a place to stay. A Mrs. Joorst."

He went to the window. Ruth followed him. He tried to look outside, but darkness had fallen, and all he could see were the rain-streaked reflections of Ruth and himself and the potted plants on the windowsill. "Can't even see the canal," he observed.

"It's still there. . . . Listen to the rain."

"Where, exactly, are we? Which canal is it? There was a hotel—"

"It's such a lovely sound. . . . The Noorder Amstel Canal. That's Apollo Laan on the other side, the Park Avenue of Amsterdam. And the Hilton—"

"That's it. The Hilton. It comes back to me now." He was silent for a moment. "If you took a room there and then gave me the key . . . . I mean, if the room were in your name . . . No, I don't suppose that would be such a good idea."

"I don't think it'll be necessary. Beatrix was fairly certain. The rain—doesn't it give you the feeling that there's nobody else in the whole world? Just the two of us here in this apartment all by ourselves."

He put his arm around her protectively. He didn't have the feeling that the two of them were all by themselves. He had the feeling that there was an enemy lurking outside. "Come away from the window," he said.

They went back to where they'd been sitting. He folded the afghan and put it on the table, then dropped into the chair. Memories of the terminal at the Hook began to play tag in his head. Why, he asked himself, had he been attacked at that particular place? Why hadn't he been attacked in London? He'd had the money in his apartment overnight. A simple burglary would have been easier, and probably more successful.

"He wanted me to get the money out of England," he mused aloud.

"What?" said Ruth.

"Nothing. I was just thinking." He looked up and saw her gazing at him. "Nothing," he said again.

"You know, don't you?" she asked.

"Know?"

"Who tried to rob you."

"I got a look at him and I think I'd recognize him if I saw him again, but I'm not sure. It's not him, though; it's who's in back of him. . . . The sherry."

"What?"

"Nothing. I just recalled something." He didn't explain, but he went on recalling.

"John," Ruth said presently, "what would happen if—well, you forgot about the whole thing? There's no proof, is there? I mean, suppose you simply went back to England, or came to Germany with me. We'd find a way."

"You mean, and leave the money here?" Cochran smiled.

"Yes."

"Within twenty-four hours half the police in Europe would be looking for me. The man the money belongs to would claim I stole it."

"Could he? After all, *he* did something illegal too. It seems to me he's in no position to call the police."

Cochran shook his head. "He could claim I stole the money in England and brought it over here on my own. Besides, the money would be discovered sometime Sunday. Or at least the suitcase would. And pretty soon—"

"But there's nothing to link it to you, is there?"

He considered. "Fingerprints, I suppose. It's not that, though. The man who arranged everything—he'd—well, he'd set off a manhunt. And even if nothing could be proved, I'm not in any position to explain myself. You don't seem to understand that, Ruth."

"I understand it. But Todd—"

"You're not being realistic. No, I have to finish what I started. That's my only hope."

She sighed.

"Otherwise I wouldn't be safe in England—or in Germany either."

"And you think you'll be safe if you do?"

"I don't know. Possibly. Or possibly not."

"But that's exactly what I'm saying. As long as there's a risk either way, you might as well go forward rather than backward."

He looked at her. "And what would happen to you? Even if no one found me—and the chances are a million to one that someone would—do you think you could go ahead working on the research you have to do, go ahead with your career? You'd be harboring a fugitive, for Christ's sake! I guess I shouldn't have come here. I guess I—" He broke off. "I hear footsteps." He sprang to his feet.

"It's probably Beatrix," Ruth said.

A key scraped in the lock. Cochran stepped in front of Ruth, to shield her. But she'd been right. It was Beatrix.

"Ah," Beatrix said, "our guest is awake." She furled her umbrella and put it in the stand beside the tall cabinet. "Such weather!" She began to take off her raincoat. "Everything is arranged."

Cochran relaxed. "I'm afraid I've put you to an awful lot of trouble."

She hung the coat in the closet. "A lot? No, just a little. I believe that none of us would be in any danger if you remained here, but I do not believe that you do. So—" she smiled—"I made a call upon a friend. Mevrouw Joorst. She owns many apartments. And you have a place in which to sleep. There is no furniture, however; it will be necessary for you to sleep on the floor. But you will certainly be out of danger."

"You're really very kind," Cochran said.

Beatrix's smile broadened. "I know. It is one of my failings." She became serious again. Mrs. Joorst, she explained, was a woman of considerable wealth. She already owned more than seventy apartments. Her son was an architect, and she was making use of his talents. The Dutch government gave advantageous loans to people who were willing to buy and restore the historic old houses along the canals in Amsterdam Centrum, for the houses were on the verge of collapsing from age and neglect. Mrs. Joorst and her son were among those who were availing themselves of the loans. They had remodeled almost an entire block of houses on the Heren Gracht into luxury apartments for foreign executives of the many multinational corporations that had branches in Holland. Mrs. Joorst was an enterprising woman and had excellent contacts within the corporations. Now she and her son were doing two more buildings. The apartments were not yet finished, but she would be pleased to let a friend of Beatrix's sleep in one of them. "It was," Beatrix concluded, "merely a matter of asking her properly."

"You're a darling!" Ruth exclaimed.

Beatrix shrugged. "I must go into the kitchen, or we will have no dinner." She turned to Cochran. "After dinner I will drive you to where you will sleep. You will be quite undisturbed there, I can assure you."

Garwood gazed toward Reijnier Vinkeles Kade. Can't see a bloody thing, he thought.

He felt unsettled. He'd been feeling unsettled for several hours, and he didn't know why. It couldn't be because of the weather, he thought, for as things had turned out, the rain and fog were fortunate—a stroke of good luck to counteract the bad. Yet a nagging anxiety persisted.

The money was almost certainly at the railway station, in a storage locker or in the left-luggage room. It was odd that Cochran hadn't been carrying it on his person. The one possibility that O'Rourke hadn't considered, that he himself hadn't considered. Apparently, without telling Arlen, Cochran had changed his method. But that didn't matter now. All that mattered was that Cochran expected to meet Peter at the railway station and to give him the money. But instead of Peter . . .

Garwood pressed his lower lip between his teeth and again tried to pinpoint the cause of his uneasiness. He reviewed his conversation with Peter. Peter had said that he couldn't leave Geneva because of the weather, because it was snowing. He'd told Peter . . .

Suddenly he realized his mistake.

He hurried to the telephone. "I'd like to place a call to Geneva," he told the operator. "To a Mr. Peter Evans, at the Hôtel Richemond."

The operator said she would ring him when the call went through.

He hung up and waited. Peter probably hadn't caught the mistake. Nevertheless, it was essential to be certain.

The telephone rang.

"I am sorry," the operator reported, "but the Hôtel Richemond informs that Mr. Evans is no longer there. He departed an hour ago."

Garwood put the telephone down. But presently he picked it up again and asked to be connected with Mr. Kenneth O'Rourke.

"Come to my room," he told O'Rourke. "We have plans to make."

37

Cochran slid his arm from under the down-filled comforter and tried to read the dial of his watch, but the light was too faint. All he could see in the pale glow cast by the street-lamp outside were strange shadows on the wall and ceiling. The shadows were those of the tree in front of the building, and they moved slowly back and forth as the tree swayed in the wind.

He listened. The rain had stopped, but the wind had risen. One of the tall windows creaked. The sound it made was irregular and mournful.

Propping himself up on one elbow, Cochran looked at Ruth. She was sleeping soundly, the comforter pulled up to her chin. She had made a sleeping bag of the two comforters and pillows Beatrix had insisted they bring with them, and her last words before falling asleep had been, "Isn't it lovely?" Uttered with a contented sigh.

Yes, he now replied silently. It's lovely.

And it would continue to be lovely. Because Beatrix had convinced him that he'd been wrong.

Carefully he pushed the comforter aside, tucked it around Ruth and got to his feet. The room was unheated, and the air was very cold. He found his coat in the heap of clothing on the floor, put it on and, fastening the belt tightly, went to the window. Holding his arm up to the glass, he again consulted his watch. Twenty minutes to six. Plenty of time. He shoved his hands into the pockets of his coat and stood there looking out, feeling calm and resolute. He might not be able to marry her; he might eventually be found and sent to jail; but he would never leave her voluntarily. And even if he went to jail, it wouldn't be forever. After serving his sentence, he would be released and he would come back to her.

He'd reached a turning point and made the turn he'd never expected to make, but now—now he was happy.

Staring at the silvery patches made by the streetlamps on the ruffled water of the Heren Gracht, he recalled what Beatrix had said.

Mrs. Joorst had waited for them. She was a slender woman who was, Cochran judged, in her early sixties. Her white hair was neatly coifed, and she was wearing beautifully tailored beige slacks and a brown cashmere turtleneck sweater. Everything about her suggested money—old money. Her features, her bearing, her clothes, her pearls. Everything except the sneakers on her feet, which were covered with the marble dust that coated everything in the foyer and the stairwell and proclaimed that she was as much construction foreman as aristocrat.

Her English was adequate, although she kept apologizing for it, and her enthusiasm for the work she was doing was irresistible. This, she said, was the finest of all the projects she'd been engaged on, the brightest jewel among all her properties. When completed, it would be *groot luxe.*

Ignoring the armload of comforters and pillows that Cochran was carrying, she insisted on his accompanying the rest of them on a tour of the premises, and as they made their way up flights of stairs and along corridors he found himself agreeing that the property really was going to be a jewel. Marble foyer and stairwells, glass-enclosed elevator shaft, tiled fireplaces, sunken tubs—the interior of the centuries-old house would indeed, when refinished, be handsome. But the job was far from complete. The elevator cage was in the shaft, but wasn't yet working; the bathroom plumbing was usable, but the kitchen appliances hadn't even been delivered; the bottom of the air shafts, which according to Mrs. Joorst would serve as patios, with potted trees and plants, were piled with lumber and slabs of marble; the light fixtures for the apartments on the upper floors hadn't been shipped from the factory; and the furniture, which Mrs. Joorst said was the most expensive she'd ever bought for her apartments, was stored in a warehouse.

Although the rooms on the top three floors couldn't be lit, she took them through those also, pointing out with the beam of her flashlight the features that would make her building superior to any other of its sort in Amsterdam. But finally she brought them back to the apartment on the first floor that she'd set aside for Mijnheer Cochran and his wife, showed them around and explained that she had to leave; she was obliged to pay a call on the head carpenter and persuade him to return to work the next morning. They'd quarreled earlier, and he'd walked off the job—"Indonesian, you know. Much skill, but most sensitive."

"Wife?" Cochran said to Beatrix when Mrs. Joorst was gone.

Beatrix shrugged. "I thought it best."

He glanced at Ruth. Evidently she and Beatrix had decided that she was to spend the night with him.

"I haven't gone camping in years," Ruth said quickly.

She would be safe enough, he thought. And he wanted her very much. Nevertheless . . . "The trouble is—" he began, intending to say that the trouble wasn't with her staying but with his leaving.

"Come," Beatrix interrupted, taking his arm. "I will show you something."

She led him to one of the front windows. The fog was lifting, but the rain was coming down as hard as ever. "That," she said, indicating the canal, "is the Heren Gracht. Unfortunately you cannot see it very well this evening, but it is one of the most beautiful canals in the city. It is also very old. The house we are in, the houses around us, the neighborhood—all are very old." She paused. "Many generations have lived and died here. Many generations. That, I think, is important for you to know."

He gave her a quizzical look.

Still holding his arm, she pointed with a finger of her free hand. "The next canal is Keizers Gracht, and the one beyond that is Prinsen Gracht. Much has occurred on all of them. On Prinsen Gracht, a walk of only five minutes from where we are, is the house in which Anne Frank lived. That, too, I think you should know."

Cochran said nothing.

"Often I walk along these canals," Beatrix continued. "I reflect. Even during the occupation, people fell in love, people married."

Ruth joined them at the window. She too looked out at the canal.

"Do you know the date on which the Franks were arrested by the Gestapo?" Beatrix asked. "It was the fourth of August, 1944. I was not acquainted with the Franks and did not for some years learn what happened at 263 Prinsen Gracht on August 4, 1944. But I remember the week very well, because on July 30, 1944, I was told that my husband had been killed.

He was one of thirty hostages who were shot as an act of reprisal. We had been married for six weeks. I was eighteen."

Cochran glanced at her. She was standing very straight now, her hands at her sides. She seemed to be addressing herself not to him or to Ruth but to the panes of glass in front of her.

"Life," Beatrix concluded, "is uncertain. I often reflect on that as I walk beside these old canals and imagine the many generations that previously walked beside them. . . . Life is uncertain; one must enjoy it as much as possible." She turned her back on the window and faced Cochran. "Do you feel what I am saying?"

Cochran nodded.

No one spoke.

Beatrix sat down on the windowsill. She appeared to be studying the bare room. "This apartment," she said at last, "it will be attractive." She paused. "Enjoy life as much as possible, John."

There was another silence. Ruth took Cochran's hand.

Beatrix sighed. "I did not marry again. Instead, I became a scholar. Now I have regrets. I should have done both."

"My situation is different," Cochran said.

"No, my dear John, it is the same. I was angry, you are angry. Anger prevents people from living their lives well. Ruth has told me about your life in London. It is dry."

"I'm in no position to change it."

"I disagree. You must not be afraid to challenge the unknown."

"I'm always challenging the unknown. That's the whole damn trouble."

"Always?" Beatrix shook her head. "No, you only did it once. You took a brave step, and perhaps one that was justified, but it was also selfish. And because it ended in tragedy, you are too angry to take another."

Cochran disengaged his hand from Ruth's and went over

to the fireplace. There were several leftover tiles on the mantel, he noticed. He stared at them. Beatrix was right, he thought. But then again . . .

"Well," Beatrix said, "I must be going. I will leave you two alone."

Cochran and Ruth went to the door with her. She kissed Ruth on the cheek and shook hands with Cochran. "Perhaps," she told him with a smile, "what I have said will be, in the end, unnecessary. What happened to you this morning may, I think, force you to reconsider your plans. But I could be mistaken. In either case, good night and good luck."

Germany, he thought. An entirely new life.

It seemed so simple now, so right. He wondered why it had seemed impossible before.

There would be problems, of course. The flat in London, Arlen, the expiration of his passport. But the problems could be solved. The money he had in Switzerland—it wasn't enough, but it would help. He would have no more difficulty in getting a new passport at the American Embassy in Bonn than he would at the Embassy in London. Arlen—well, so what? Arlen would simply have to get himself another courier.

And there was the money due him from Evans. It would last for a while.

Kitty and Ian could dispose of the flat. There was really nothing in it that he wanted to keep.

A year in Munich. And after that—would he dare return to the States? He would have to think about it. Ruth's lawyer might be able to accomplish something, after all; it would depend on that.

He shivered, and drew the belt of his coat even more tightly around him. He thought about the many generations that had occupied the houses along the Heren Gracht.

38

Klaus Ranken turned on the light in the kitchen and began to search for the coffee pot. The kitchen wasn't his domain, and he felt awkward in it. But his wife was still asleep, and he'd been awake for what seemed like hours. Unable to stay in bed any longer, he'd decided to begin his day early.

He found the coffee pot and began opening the doors of various cabinets. He explored each shelf. The coffee wasn't on any of them. He gave up; he'd have milk instead. When he opened the refrigerator to get the milk, however, he found the coffee. Ridiculous, he thought; coffee doesn't spoil. But evidently his wife had some theory about it. On the subject of food, she had many theories. Beside the jar of coffee was a container of yogurt. He took that out of the refrigerator also.

Waiting for the water to boil, he walked into the dining room and turned on the light. According to the tall clock in the corner, it was thirty-one minutes past six, and if that was what the clock said, that was the exact time. The clock was never wrong. He'd bought it in a secondhand shop and sent it to a friend of his to be repaired. The friend had done a remarkable job. Although the clock was a hundred and seventy-five—no, a hundred and seventy-seven—years old, it kept absolutely perfect time. It had been one of the best purchases he'd ever made, that clock; he was proud of it. They didn't make clocks like that these days. Clock-making was a lost art.

He sat down at the table in the chair usually occupied by his oldest son and watched the swinging of the clock's pendulum. Its effect on him was hypnotic. His mind began to go blank. But presently he blinked and roused himself, and turned his eyes away. His mental processes returned to normal.

He dreaded what lay ahead. He would be going to the office, and there were bound to be humiliations. Some good-natured, others not. He hadn't reported for work the day before. After his two-hour session with the police, he'd passed an entirely sleepless night, and instead of going to the office as he'd planned, he'd telephoned to say that he was sick. Now he would have to explain his sickness along with everything else. And there would be those who didn't believe him.

But the ticking of the clock reassured him. This day would pass. This week would pass. This year. The mistake of Baden-Baden would be forgotten and forgiven. If there was anything that needed to be forgiven. And in point of fact, there wasn't. It wasn't his fault that the poor woman from Karlsruhe had been murdered. All he'd done was befriend a foreigner and invite him to go to the Casino. A nice-looking foreigner, at that. Nothing in the least sinister about him.

If I had it to do over again, he thought defiantly, I would do the same thing. I like people. I like foreigners. I'm cosmopolitan in my tastes.

Furthermore, there was no proof that Howard—or O'Rourke, as the police called him—had killed the unfortunate Erika Rebholz. There was little doubt, of course, that he'd stolen Ganzhorn's car. But the only link between the theft of the car and the murder was a complicated business involving registration plates, for which there could be many explanations.

And Ranken had cooperated with the police fully. In fact, they'd been most favorably impressed by the accuracy of his description of O'Rourke. They'd said so. "I have an artist's eye," he'd replied. And this was no less than the truth.

If Fräulein Rebholz had had any contact with a terrorist group, the entire matter would be understandable. The police were investigating this possibility, they'd admitted. But they'd also admitted that their preliminary findings revealed nothing of that sort. Fräulein Rebholz had been, it appeared, simply a secretary and a music-lover. After work on Thursday she'd had dinner with friends and attended a concert. Then she and her friends had stopped for a glass of beer. It had been a long walk from the bar to the Tiefgarage. There had been nothing unusual about the evening, and there was, as far as the police could determine, nothing unusual about Fräulein Rebholz's life except, perhaps, its dullness.

In addition, there was no indication that she'd been sexually molested. She'd been, apparently, one of those rare creatures who at forty-three are still virgins.

Based on what the police were willing to confide in Ranken, he could only conclude that the murder of Erika Rebholz was a crime without a motive; and that, as such, it might never be solved.

The police themselves had expressed no optimism, and Ranken could understand why. Automobile theft was so common that all the police in Europe couldn't control it, and a large percentage of the stolen cars were never found. But murder was less common. Murderers were apprehended more often than not. The difficulty in this particular case, they'd said, was the international nature of it. The police had no positive evidence that O'Rourke had stolen the car, and only the merest suspicion that he'd killed Fräulein Rebholz. They simply wanted to question him, and if he was already back in England it might not be possible for them to do so. They couldn't extradite him without having a much stronger case than they had. The British authorities would cooperate, of course, but the British authorities had their own problems. Nevertheless, information had been sent to Interpol and also to Scotland Yard—O'Rourke's name and passport number, along with the details, such as they were, of the crimes that the Germans wanted to question him about. If he was back in England, he would eventually be visited by Scotland Yard investigators. If. And even then it would take time. The policemen who had interviewed Ranken didn't have his cosmopolitan viewpoint, it seemed. They'd never been to England, as he had. Their opinion of British law-enforcement was low. "The British will only begin their inquiries," one of them had said, "after they've had their tea."

Yet apparently they weren't entirely pessimistic, either. For they'd instructed him to keep them informed of his whereabouts. Considering his excellent description of O'Rourke, they might want to call upon him to make an identification. They wouldn't have said that, Ranken reasoned, if they hadn't felt there was *some* possibility of their locating O'Rourke.

And he fervently hoped that they did. If only to prove his own innocence. For while the police hadn't expressed, or even hinted at, a belief in his complicity, it had crossed his mind that they might be harboring such a belief.

Shaking his head sadly, he went back to the kitchen. The coffee wasn't ready. He stood beside the counter top and waited.

He was still waiting when the telephone rang.

He hurried into the hall to answer it.

"Herr Ranken," said the voice at the other end of the line, "Braun here." Braun was one of the police officers who had interviewed him.

"Yes, sir," Ranken said nervously.

"We would like to know where you can be reached today."

Ranken's heart began to hammer. "Yes, sir. Of course, sir. Has something happened? Would you like me to come to your office?"

As soon as he'd uttered the second question, he regretted it. A visit to police headquarters was the last thing in the world he wanted.

But there was no need for anxiety, he learned presently. The news was good. Word had just been received from England that the subject of the German inquiry, Kenneth O'Rourke, had been found to have left his flat on Wednesday afternoon and not been seen since. Further investigation revealed that passage had been booked in the subject's name on the Sealink steamer to Holland for Wednesday night. Dutch authorities reported that his landing card had been turned in at the Hook of Holland on Thursday morning. The British suggested that the Germans contact the Dutch.

The Germans had immediately done so.

"It is possible," Braun concluded, "that we will learn of his whereabouts within hours."

Ranken said, "But he landed yesterday. He might be anywhere in Europe by now. Anywhere in the world, even." Silently he damned the British and their tea. He had a fleeting vision of a vast hall filled with policemen, all drinking tea.

"Schiphol was closed yesterday," Braun said. "Either he is traveling by surface or he is still in Holland. We have requested Holland to check hotel registrations. Also we have requested the same from Switzerland, Belgium, France and Denmark. Depending on the cooperation we receive, and on our luck, we may have Herr O'Rourke located by the end of the day. Even earlier, perhaps. Where can you be reached, in case we want you to identify a photograph?"

Ranken gave the police officer his business telephone number.

His heart was still hammering when he returned to the kitchen. But with excitement rather than dread.

39

The newspaper stand was closed, the lobby was deserted, there was no one at the registration desk. O'Rourke rapped on the counter. A clerk emerged from behind the mailboxes. "I wish to settle my bill," O'Rourke said.

The clerk referred him to the cashier, whose station was round the corner. Humming, O'Rourke paid for his room nd left the building.

There were no taxis. The doorman telephoned for one. O'Rourke waited at the top of the steps. The air was much older than it had been the night before, and the wind was trong. But the sky had cleared; several stars were visible. It was ten minutes to seven. The sun, he estimated, wouldn't come up for at least an hour and a half.

The doorman reported that a taxi would be along shortly. O'Rourke offered him a cigarette. The doorman declined. O'Rourke took one himself and inquired about taxis in general. He'd discovered the preceding evening, he said, that Amster-

dam was different from London; in Amsterdam, taxi driver
weren't allowed to pick up passengers except at designated
points—was that correct? The doorman said that it was. In
that case, O'Rourke asked, where, in the central district, were
the designated points situated? There were several, the doorman replied: the railroad station, Leidse Plein, Dam Square
to name but three.

"Leidse Plein? Dam Square?" O'Rourke opened the map
he'd picked up at the Avis counter in the lobby the night
before. "Show me."

They moved closer to the light. The doorman indicated
the location of the Hilton, as well as the other places he'd
mentioned. O'Rourke thanked him and continued to study
the map until the taxi arrived.

He told the driver to take him to the Centraal Station.
The trip took fifteen minutes. When they reached the station,
O'Rourke observed that the state of affairs he'd found at
eight o'clock at night also existed at a quarter past seven in
the morning: there were more passengers than taxis at the
taxi rank. Apparently it was like that all the time, he concluded,
thanks to the bloody union. He'd been correct in telling Garwood that the best means of getting quickly away from the
station was on foot or by tram.

His tour of the interior of the station was perfunctory.
He'd spent almost an hour there with Garwood; the details
were fixed in his mind. Nevertheless he walked as far as the
platform on which the Holland-Italy Express would come in,
and reviewed his plan. He foresaw no problem. Then, in the
concourse, he studied the map again. There was no scale on
it, but he guessed at the distance between the station and
Dam Square: less than a mile. Leidse Plein was three times
that far, and the Hilton was twice as far as Leidse Plein.

Satisfied, he left the station and went into the Tourist Information Center, which was housed in a small building outside the station's main entrance. He noticed the large number

of trams lined up in the station square. It appeared that every tramline in the city either passed the square or terminated at it. He questioned an attendant, hoping that she spoke English, and found that she did. She explained that the number-nine tram was the one that stopped at Dam Plein. The service was very frequent. The fare was one guilder. She pointed out the stall at which he could buy a ticket; it was only a few yards away. Or, she added, he could buy a ticket on the tram itself. A ticket was good for one hour on any line.

Seven minutes later, he heard Dam Plein announced over the tram's loudspeaker system, and got off.

Decidedly inferior to Trafalgar Square, he thought as he looked around, but obviously this was one of the focal points of the city. In the predawn darkness, it was difficult to identify the various buildings, and he made little effort to do so. A big hulk that might be a cathedral, a monument, a colony of pigeons were all that he noticed, although as he passed the monument he detected the faint lingering odor of marijuana. In public? he wondered. Decadent, he concluded.

The map had indicated canals to the east and to the west of Dam Plein. They ran roughly parallel to the street the tram had followed, Dam Rak. Those to the east were closer, however. Leaving the monument behind him, he headed in an easterly direction, passed the entrance to the Hotel Krasnapolsky, observed a taxi rank and turned the corner into a narrow alley called Pijlsteeg. And after a short distance he came to the first of the canals east of Dam Rak, the Oude Zijds Voorburg Wal. He turned to the right.

The street that bordered the canal was very narrow, yet parking was allowed. Cars stood side by side, facing the water and the parking meters that lined it like fenceposts. There was barely enough space between the cars and the houses on the other side of the pavement for one moving vehicle.

The houses looked old and dilapidated. There was rubbish floating in the water. This was definitely not one of Amsterdam's better neighborhoods, O'Rourke decided.

He walked slowly for a block and a half, the only perso
on the street. Some of the houses had shops on the grou
floor, others did not. The shopwindows were dark, but l
paused to study the displays anyway. Some of them featur
pornographic literature and sex devices. Not like Soh
O'Rourke thought, but in their own way interesting. Abo
one of the shops he noticed a red light in the window. F
paused. Could it be . . . ? He stepped into the middle
the pavement and looked around more carefully. On the fir
floor of a building across the canal he saw another red ligh
A slow smile creased his face. What he'd heard about Amste
dam was true. There was a "district." But at this hour
the morning? Either some of the girls had forgotten to tu
off their lights, or times were very hard.

A man on a bicycle came around a corner and pedal
toward him. O'Rourke stepped out of the way. The cycli
passed. A moment later, O'Rourke's ears picked up soun
he hadn't heard before. The sounds were quite near. He we
to investigate, and found an elderly man hunched over besi
one of the parking meters, vomiting.

Drunk, thought O'Rourke. Disgusting.

But as he watched the man, his eyes took in details l
hadn't seen before. A rail ran along the edge of the pavemen
to keep cars from rolling into the water. The rail was ank
high. O'Rourke peered down. The drop from the road t
the water was three or four feet. The water, illuminated a
intervals by the streetlamps, appeared to be oily and unclea

He began to hum. A most unsanitary city, really. But
had its merits.

He made his way back to the middle of the road and retrace
his steps to Dam Square.

A taxi took him from the Krasnapolsky to the Hilton. B
the time he reached the Hilton, the sun was up.

At a quarter to nine, Garwood appeared in the lobby. 'Ready?" he asked.

"Naturally," O'Rourke replied.

"Then let's go."

"No hurry," O'Rourke said, and with deliberate insouciance he stopped to light a cigarette before going to the door.

This time there were two taxis waiting near the entrance. The doorman gave a signal, and one of the taxis pulled up. O'Rourke and Garwood got in. Garwood told the driver to take them to Centraal Station.

Traffic was heavier now. The ride took twenty minutes. Garwood kept looking at his watch. To the extent that his expression revealed anything, it revealed a scarcely contained anger that could erupt at any moment. But, O'Rourke was learning, that was the lawyer's usual expression; it didn't signify anything in particular. During the past twenty-four hours, his opinion of Garwood had undergone revision, downward. For all that Garwood had accomplished on Trumper's behalf, the man was a proper bastard. Even more cold-blooded than O'Rourke had at first thought. Even more slippery, too. Garwood probably wouldn't have lifted a finger to help Trumper if Trumper's grandfather hadn't been a member of the peerage. Besides, it wasn't Garwood who had got Trumper acquitted, but the barrister who had argued the case in court. And the barrister had most likely collected the larger fee, as well.

He smiled to himself. Furthermore, Garwood had a limited imagination.

"Stop humming!" Garwood snapped.

O'Rourke was startled. He hadn't realized that he was humming. He stopped, resentfully. He didn't like being spoken to in that tone of voice. But his resentment subsided when he realized that the tone of voice was a clue to Garwood's state of mind. Despite his cold-bloodedness, the lawyer was nervous.

Inexperienced, O'Rourke thought. Not a man of action

He began to hum again, but caught himself. He could understand Garwood's uneasiness. Garwood had admitted that he couldn't be sure the informer would be on the train. He'd merely made an educated guess, after learning that this was the only direct overnight train from˙ Switzerland to Amsterdam. Besides, there was the size of the crowd on the platform to be considered; too large a crowd would complicate matters

But while O'Rourke was aware of the uncertainties, he didn't feel that there was anything to worry about. He had the conviction that all would turn out well. What he was experiencing, instead of anxiety, was a tension, a sort of excitement, that was almost pleasant.

The taxi pulled up at the side entrance to the station. Garwood got out and paid the driver. "Hurry," he said to O'Rourke.

O'Rourke consulted his watch. Exactly nine thirty. The train, according to Garwood, was due at nine thirty-seven They had only seven minutes in which to cover a considerable distance; but it annoyed O'Rourke to be told to hurry, so he stopped to light another cigarette and went into the station as slowly as if they had all the time in the world.

The large concourse was more crowded now than it had been earlier. People were going in all directions. O'Rourke wasn't distracted, however. With Garwood at his side, urging him to walk more quickly, he moved across the concourse at a deliberate pace, directly toward the underpass that ran beneath the platforms.

"You're sure you'll recognize him?" Garwood asked when they reached the two long flights of stairs that led, like a pair of upstretched arms, to the platform at which the Holland-Italy Express was scheduled to come in.

O'Rourke looked at him. The lawyer's face had turned grayer than his hair, and something had happened to the nerves of his face; the muscles beside his right eye and the right corner of his mouth were twitching. Like someone who's about to have a fit, O'Rourke thought. "Naturally," he said with scorn.

"Well, then . . ." Garwood turned and went up the stairway to their left.

O'Rourke went up the other one.

There were only a few people on the platform. O'Rourke glanced in both directions. Although the train was due in one minute, there was no sign of it. But he observed that one of the signal lights in the distance was green. Discarding the stub of his cigarette, he looked toward where Garwood should be, and saw him emerge from the staircase. There were less than fifty yards between them.

Watching Garwood, O'Rourke felt a new wave of contempt. No sooner had he set foot on the platform than the lawyer jammed his hands into the pockets of his overcoat and started to pace. Three slow strides in one direction, three in the other. Scared, thought O'Rourke. The old hawk has turned into a nervous little sparrow.

O'Rourke stiffened as his ears picked up a sound. He strained his eyes and saw the train come around a bend. He took a deep breath and began to hum.

The noise grew louder as the train drew closer. O'Rourke kept his eyes on it unwaveringly. Presently the engine screeched past him, decelerating. Then the baggage cars. And finally the Wagon-Lits, some of them still with ice on their roofs. As they rolled to a halt, he could see passengers taking their suitcases off the racks.

The car in front of O'Rourke expelled a jet of steam. The doors at the ends of the cars opened. Passengers began to alight. O'Rourke's eyes narrowed. So did his thoughts. He concentrated on remembering one face.

There were fewer people getting off the train than he'd expected—evidently it hadn't been booked to capacity. He scanned the faces of those nearest him, then looked beyond them. He could see ten, fifteen, twenty faces at a glance.

But the face of the man he was looking for wasn't among them.

He swung around to check on Garwood. The lawyer was standing near the top of the other staircase, watching the passengers who were approaching from the rear of the train. He seemed to be meeting with no success either. But just as O'Rourke was about to turn away, the lawyer did an about face and started toward him, beckoning.

O'Rourke ran to where Garwood was.

"He's coming," Garwood said breathlessly.

"Righto," said O'Rourke, and took over Garwood's position. Garwood started down the stairs.

O'Rourke picked out the man he'd followed from Carey Street to the Victoria Air Terminal. Wearing a tan raincoat and carrying a small black suitcase, the man was some sixty feet away, coming toward him with an uncertain gait and looking about dazedly, as if he couldn't quite believe that the train had arrived.

O'Rourke's gaze darted toward the staircase. What he saw reassured him. The descending passengers were spaced well apart. Humming softly, he waited until the man in the tan raincoat reached the top of the stairs, then came up beside him.

Evans stepped off with his left foot. O'Rourke put his own left foot in front of Evans's right and gave him a violent push between the shoulderblades.

The result exceeded anything he'd anticipated. Evans pitched forward and uttered a shrill cry. The suitcase flew from his hand. His arms flailed, then shot forward to break his fall. But his head struck the edge of a step before his hands. He did a half-somersault, fell sideways, rolled down two more steps and lay inert.

O'Rourke retreated to the platform, walked around to the other staircase and went down to the underpass. A crowd

as already collecting at the spot where Evans was sprawled.
'Rourke decided to have a closer look.

Noting the peculiar angle of Evans's head, he was aston-
ied. He'd achieved more than he'd intended.

Garwood was waiting at the end of the underpass.

"A piece of cake," O'Rourke informed him. "I think he
oke his neck."

Garwood's face went white. "You mean he's . . . dead?"

"Suspect so."

Garwood swayed.

O'Rourke took his arm. "Let's move," he said, and hustled
arwood across the concourse.

A number-nine tram was arriving. O'Rourke pulled Gar-
ood toward it, and they climbed aboard. O'Rourke gave
ie motorman two guilders and pushed Garwood into a seat.
arwood began to tremble.

"What's bothering you?" O'Rourke asked impatiently.
You got your money's worth, didn't you?"

Garwood nodded. He seemed to have lost the ability to
peak.

The tram started. Through the rear window O'Rourke
atched the station recede.

At Dam Plein he tugged at Garwood's sleeve and led him
the exit. They descended to the street. The tram continued
1 its route.

"Now," O'Rourke said to the lawyer, "I'll show you a lovely
x shop."

The two policemen arrived at the Hilton at nine forty one, parked their car in the parking area and got out. The dark-haired one, Joop Toepels, took a handkerchief from his pocket and, leaning against the car, blew his nose.

"With such a cold," said his partner, Cornelis Brondel, "you should have stayed home."

Joop shoved the handkerchief back into his pocket and sighed. "I know." He was prone to respiratory ailments, and this cold, he could already tell, was going to be a bad one. "It was the rain yesterday." He'd got wet, and the symptoms had manifested themselves within hours. Shortly after midnight he'd awakened with a cough and the beginning of a sore throat. Now he felt as if he was running a temperature.

They crossed the driveway and started up the steps.

"Otherwise," Cornelis added, "it's liable to spoil your Christmas."

"As far as I'm concerned," Joop said, "that's already spoiled. My wife's parents are coming."

Cornelis nodded understandingly. He didn't like his wife's family either. Especially her brother Henri.

They entered the lobby and, bypassing the registration desk, headed for the manager's office. They'd had dealings with the manager before. He was properly discreet.

His secretary told them that he was on the telephone. They waited. Joop sneezed and blew his nose again. His nose, Cornelis observed, was beginning to turn red.

"He's free now," the secretary said.

They went into the manager's private office. He greeted them without getting up from his desk and said, "And what may I do for you gentlemen this morning?"

Joop took the notebook from his pocket and consulted it. "Among your guests is a certain Kenneth O'Rourke. British. Your records show that he registered yesterday. Do you want his passport number?"

The manager shook his head.

"We would like his room number."

"Something serious?" the manager asked.

Joop sneezed.

"Questioning," Cornelis replied tersely. "We are instructed to bring him to Marnixstraat."

The manager raised his eyebrows. Marnixstraat was the location of police headquarters, so the matter was obviously not a trivial one. He picked up the telephone, dialed, identified himself to the party who answered, and requested the room number of O'Rourke, Kenneth. While waiting for a reply, he studied the notes on his desk calendar. His expression betrayed no emotion. "I see," he said presently. "Very well. Thank you." He put down the telephone and turned to the policemen. "I'm afraid I can't help you gentlemen. Mijnheer O'Rourke checked out several hours ago. At six forty-seven, to be exact."

"Would anyone know where he went?" Joop asked.

He expected a negative answer and he received one.

Cornelis asked that they be shown the room O'Rourke had occupied. The manager himself took them to it.

But the room had already been made up. There was nothing of O'Rourke's in it.

The policemen spoke to the chambermaid. She too, she said, had found nothing of consequence in the room. Waste-basket empty, wardrobe empty, but an unusually large number of cigarette butts in the ashtrays. She'd flushed them down the toilet.

Cornelis thanked her, and the two policemen returned to the lobby with the manager. The manager seemed relieved.

On the way back to their car, the policemen questioned the doorman, who remembered that a man who was either British or American had left by taxi at approximately seven o'clock. The doorman wasn't sure of the man's destination, but he did recall that the man had inquired about the location of taxi stands in the central district.

Cornelis radioed the results of their investigation to head-quarters. The message was acknowledged, and Cornelis and Joop were told to return to headquarters.

"I wonder where he went so early in the morning," Cornelis said as he guided the car out of the parking lot.

"Who knows?" Joop said irritably. "It's not our concern. Let the Germans worry about it. He hasn't committed any crime in Holland." He began to cough. "Have we time to stop for a cup of coffee?"

"A what?" Garwood asked.

"A sex shop," O'Rourke replied. He was amused by the look of horror on the lawyer's face. The old man was apparently beginning to recover; he'd stopped trembling and found his voice. He was still pale, however. "You know: magazines, books, naked girls, naked boys, peepshows. Come now, don't tell me you've never been to a sex shop."

"You're mad," said Garwood.

O'Rourke smiled. "Mad, am I? Come now, Mr. Solicitor. I'm not the one who arranged this little holiday. *You* are. If you don't like the way it's developing, that's not my fault. I'm merely doing what you're paying me to do."

Garwood shook his head. "Utterly mad."

"Come now," O'Rourke said. "You're having a grand time. You know you are."

"You just . . . killed a man."

"I simply gave him a bit of a push. I can't help it that he didn't know how to fall. He probably hadn't had much experience with falling." O'Rourke's smile faded. "You know what I think? I think you're actually pleased. I don't think you plan to turn the money over to a client at all. I think you plan to keep it." He took Garwood's arm, firmly. "Come along, this way. It isn't far. The fresh air will do you a world of good. You're looking liverish."

Garwood tried to extricate his arm, but O'Rourke held on and said, "You sit in your office all day, thinking, thinking, thinking about what other people should do. It isn't good for you. You ought to get out more, get more exercise, more fresh air. Take a deep breath now, a nice deep breath. The fresh air is healthy."

"Release my arm, O'Rourke."

"A nice deep breath."

"I wish to return to the hotel."

O'Rourke tightened his grip. "What will you do at the hotel? Simply make yourself nervous, which isn't good for you, now, is it? Besides, there's hardly enough time. No, much better that you should stay out in the fresh air, at least until you've settled down a bit. You can return to the hotel after you have the money. Meanwhile, the less time you spend at the hotel, the better for both of us."

"You're hurting me. Release my arm, or I'll cause a disturbance. The police will come."

"Will they, now? Well, that's exactly what I'm afraid will happen if you return to the hotel. No, sir, Mr. Solicitor, I have no intention of letting you go back to the hotel. I intend to keep you with me until after twelve o'clock, until you have your money and I have mine."

"If it's the money you want—" Garwood stopped abruptly.

"Yes?"

Garwood pursed his lips. He seemed to be thinking.

O'Rourke's smile returned. He knew exactly what thoughts were passing through Garwood's mind. The lawyer was torn between the desire to pay now and get rid of him and the fear that if he did, O'Rourke would take the money and run

eaving him to deal with the American himself. "Yes?" he
aid again.

"Nothing," Garwood muttered. "Perhaps you're right."

"Of course I'm right. Now come along."

"Release my arm."

O'Rourke released it. He started across Dam Rak toward
he Hotel Krasnapolsky. Garwood accompanied him. They
ust missed being hit by a north-bound tram. O'Rourke took
Garwood's arm again, but more lightly this time. "Traffic's
is bad as London," he said amiably. "And all the bicycles.
Terrible nuisance, the bicycles. The traffic too. Can you imag-
ne trying to negotiate Trafalgar Square on a bicycle? A proper
ness you'd be in, now, wouldn't you?"

"Why are we going this way?" Garwood asked. "Why don't
ve go the other way?"

"Do you own a car?"

"No longer. Where are we going?"

"You do know how to drive one, though, don't you?"

"Of course. But—"

"Splendid. But I was telling you, the traffic. And the morals.
They smoke marijuana on the street here." They passed the
hotel, and O'Rourke guided Garwood around the corner.

"Why are we going this way?" Garwood asked again.

"I'm taking you to the red-light district. It's like I was
saying, the morals here. Astonishing. Sex shops, brothels, marijuana. You should see some of the things I've seen. A dildoe
the size of a cricket bat. Amazing. Reminded me of Trumper.
But I don't suppose you know about that. Imagine—a red-
light district, in this day and age. Makes you wonder, doesn't
it?"

Garwood stopped in his tracks, causing O'Rourke to stop
also. "How do you know where the red-light district is?"

O'Rourke urged him forward again. "I was there this
morning."

Again Garwood stopped. "You were?"

"Of course. I'm an early riser. Require very little sleep. Four, five hours, that's all. Fascinating area, this. Not as lively at eight o'clock in the morning as it might be, but nevertheless . . . " He tugged on Garwood's arm.

Garwood began to walk. "But why?"

"Because we need a car, Mr. Solicitor. Because we need a *car*."

"But—"

"No buts. We *need* one. Suppose Cochran doesn't want to give you the suitcase. Suppose he resists."

"He won't resist. Evans won't be there; I will. And so will you."

"And that's the problem, as I see it. Suppose he recognizes me. I mean, there's liable to be a bit of a fuss. We need a car. Definitely."

Garwood looked at him. The color had returned to his face. He was interested.

"And," O'Rourke said, "this is where we're going to get the car."

Garwood's face clouded again. "You want to steal *another* car? Suppose you're caught. Suppose—"

"It's simple, really, when a chap knows how. And I daresay you wouldn't have hired me if you didn't think I knew how. Would you?"

They reached the canal. O'Rourke led Garwood to the right, along the narrow street he'd surveyed earlier.

"I didn't think we ought to use the car I picked up in Germany. I thought we'd best leave that at the airport. It's a different car I'm after. And as long as you know how to drive—"

"Me drive a stolen car? You're out of your mind, O'Rourke."

"Well, then, possibly I'll drive. The important thing is to have transport. See that shop over there? That's the one I was telling you about." He eased Garwood toward it.

"I'm not interested," Garwood protested.

"You should take an interest. Even at your age a man should take an interest, is the way I see it."

Reluctantly Garwood glanced at the display in the shopwindow. O'Rourke studied the street. All the parking spaces were taken, as they'd been before. There were two people walking along the opposite side of the canal, but they would soon be past. There was also a man on this side of the canal, but his back was toward O'Rourke and Garwood, and he was at least fifty yards away. The shops, as O'Rourke had anticipated, weren't yet open. This was a neighborhood that came to life at night.

He scanned the buildings. It was possible that someone might be looking out of a window. But that was a chance he'd simply have to take. "There," he said.

Garwood turned around.

O'Rourke pointed to an Opel. "The brown one."

Garwood edged away from him. O'Rourke seized his arm so tightly that Garwood gasped.

"I—I'll—"

"Shut up, you stupid sod!" O'Rourke said angrily. "We have to be quick. Do as I tell you." He pulled Garwood across the few yards of pavement to where the car was parked.

Garwood continued to resist. O'Rourke gave the arm a violent tug. Garwood stumbled against the car. It was parked beside a small green van. O'Rourke yanked the arm again, sending Garwood forward between the two vehicles. As Garwood staggered, O'Rourke released the arm and stepped behind him, taking the wrench from his pocket. He pushed Garwood ahead of him until they were partly hidden between the van and the Opel. Then, grabbing Garwood around the waist, he suddenly bent his knees. Garwood's knees buckled too, as if he were about to sit. O'Rourke brought the wrench down across the back of Garwood's head and pushed him forward. Garwood fell on his face. O'Rourke stooped and hit him again before throwing the wrench into the canal.

It took less than ten seconds to drag the body to the rail and hoist it over.

O'Rourke didn't stop running until he reached Dam Plein. Panting, he entered the lobby of the Hotel Krasnapolsky and dropped into a chair. Only then did it occur to him that he just might have cost himself nineteen hundred quid.

For several minutes, thinking of the suit, the shirt and all the incidental expenses he'd incurred and for which he might not now be reimbursed, he was extremely angry. But as his pulse returned to normal, so did his temper. It wasn't certain that Garwood had been carrying the money in his pocket; he might have been intending to pay O'Rourke from the money in the suitcase.

In point of fact, O'Rourke told himself, he'd been quite lucky. If Garwood hadn't been so shaken, it would have been more difficult to gain the upper hand. He would have managed to do it, of course; but greater effort would have been required. As it was, Garwood had been mere putty.

O'Rourke smiled. It never failed: the ones who thought themselves the smartest were invariably the most stupid.

He took a final deep breath and glanced at his watch. Not quite ten thirty. He had, at most, an hour and a half. Thrusting himself out of the chair, he crossed to the porter's desk.

"Can you tell me where I can find a department store?" he asked.

The porter considered the question for some time before replying. "There are many fine stores on Kalverstraat. What nature merchandise is it you wish to purchase?"

"Dutch nature," O'Rourke said. "Kitchenware."

"Kalverstraat," the porter said, and gave him the names of two stores.

"And where might Kalverstraat be?"

The porter whipped out a map, opened it and began with the same phrase that the doorman at the Hilton had used.

Planting his forefinger near the center of the map, he said, "We are *here*." Then he paused, moved his finger slightly and said, "Kalverstraat is *there*."

"But isn't that just across the square?" O'Rourke asked.

"Exactly," the porter said, pleased to have made himself understood the first time around.

O'Rourke took off.

And within three minutes of entering the first shop the porter had mentioned, he found precisely what he wanted: a paring knife with a five-inch steel blade.

42

Cochran kissed Ruth lightly on the forehead, the tip of the nose, the lips. She clung to him.

"Come back," she said. "Please come back."

"Count on it," he assured her.

They kissed again, and he left the apartment.

Mrs. Joorst was standing in the foyer, supervising the hanging of a chandelier. She greeted Cochran with a smile and said, "I hope that my first tenants slept well."

Cochran grinned and said, "Fine."

She nodded. "That is for me a good omen." She turned to the workman on the ladder. *"Hoger, hoger."*

The workman raised the chandelier several inches.

"Jes. Goed," said Mrs. Joorst. "One must administer everything oneself," she explained to Cochran.

"I wonder," he said, "if you can tell me how to get to the station from here."

"Centraal Station? It is but a short distance. Ten, fifteen

minutes by walking. Come." She led him to the front door, which was open, and pointed to the right. "You walk in that direction to the first street, Burgwal. There you turn to the right. After one block you come to the next canal, Singel. You cross it on the bridge, and on the other side you turn to the left. You walk along the Singel until you come to the end. There you are at Prins Hendrik Kade. You turn right, and you will see Centraal Station. Ten, fifteen minutes. But—" she indicated a blue Mercedes that was parked across the street— "if you are in a haste, I will drive you in the automobile."

"No, no," Cochran said quickly. "I've plenty of time. Thank you."

"Very well." She returned to the hanging of the chandelier.

Cochran went down the steps and turned to the right. Mrs. Joorst's words lingered with him: "That is for me a good omen." A good omen for me too, he thought. Although he was not by nature superstitious, he had a certain sense of occasion as he walked along Heren Gracht and turned the corner into Burgwal, and the idea of a good omen enhanced it.

A sense of occasion was something he rarely had. Most of the important events in his life had taken place without fanfare and had seemed, at the time, more or less logical progressions from one set of circumstances to another. His graduation from college, his marriage, his demobilization, his first day at the Treasury Department—all were turning points, but he'd not thought of them as such; he was merely doing what other people did. Even on the night he'd accepted Arlen's offer, and on the night he'd left on his first trip to Geneva, he'd had no particular awareness that he was taking a step that would irrevocably change his existence; he'd merely felt that he was doing what was necessary, and that there was nothing particularly dramatic about it.

Only once had he been conscious of doing something extraordinary, something that could never be undone. The evening he'd boarded the jet at Boston's Logan Airport, with Stephanie beside him, he'd known that nothing would ever be the same again. And as the plane had swept down the runway he'd told himself that part one of his life was coming to an end; part two was beginning. Exit Steve Donner; enter John Cochran.

That was the one time. There had never, before or since, been another.

But now he had the feeling that there was going to be more to his life than he'd expected. There was going to be a part three.

Crossing the bridge over the Singel Canal, he turned to the left. Bridges, he thought. Links from one side to another. Amsterdam was a city of bridges. It was appropriate that the new segment of his life should begin in Amsterdam.

A dinner date with Kitty he hadn't wanted to keep. An assignment from Garwood he hadn't wanted to undertake. An attack on him at the Hook of Holland that might have been fatal. And look what they had led to. Incredible.

He paused for a moment to enjoy the view. An old neighborhood. In some ways, a derelict neighborhood. But to him, just then, the most beautiful neighborhood he'd ever seen.

He glanced at his watch. A quarter to eleven. Far more time than he needed. But he'd allowed himself the extra time for a reason. He wanted to find out about the train service to Munich. As soon as he gave Evans the key to the locker, as soon as he received the money, he'd be free. Ruth and he could leave.

The key to the locker. The suitcase. The money. Some of Cochran's euphoria left him. It would have been wise, he told himself, to take out his share of the money before putting the suitcase in the locker. He'd been too rattled at the time to think of that. There was still time, however. If Evans didn't show up before noon.

But Evans might show up before noon. The train from Switzerland, Cochran recalled, arrived sometime during the midmorning. Evans might simply have chosen to wait at the station until Cochran got there.

More of Cochran's euphoria left him. His thoughts became almost black. Garwood was the one he had to worry about. The bottle of cheap sherry on the table, the hotplate, the chair with broken springs, the sweater that was coming unraveled—Garwood was a man who was hard up. He'd once had money, but he'd lost it. And in his position as custodian of other people's money, he'd probably lost theirs as well. Now, quite possibly, he was trying to recoup. Three hundred and fifty thousand pounds could mean a great deal to Garwood. It could mean the difference between continuing as a respected member of the legal profession and going under. Or, if embezzlement was involved, of going to prison.

Yes, despite his efforts to keep up appearances, Garwood was down and out.

Evans was a client, though. An old friend. Would Garwood attempt to steal from Evans? If he was desperate enough, he sure as hell would. Evans, with his gullibility, his lack of any kind of practical experience, would be the first choice.

What was puzzling, however, was the fact that the attempt to steal the money had been made in Holland. If Garwood intended to use the three hundred and fifty thousand pounds to pay back obligations he'd incurred in England, wouldn't he want the money to be available to him in England? And the theft would have been so much easier there.

Unless . . .

Was it possible?

Of course it was possible. Garwood had been planning to take the money and run. Deposit it in a Swiss bank account under his own name and then vanish. South America, the

Far East, anywhere. His wife was dead, he had no ties, he wanted to spend the last few years of his life in the luxury he'd once known. On Evans's inheritance.

But who was the young man in the suede coat? Cochran wondered.

Some thug Garwood had hired, probably. Some minor criminal. One who didn't have a prison record, no doubt, who was free to come and go without suspicion. A nobody, really.

In that case . . . Cochran felt a sudden chill. In that case, Garwood was probably in Holland at this very moment.

I'll have to warn Evans, Cochran thought, quickening his pace without realizing that he was doing so. Garwood or his hired hand might make another attempt. Perhaps in Switzerland. Perhaps even in Amsterdam, if Evans had been dumb enough to tell Garwood that he was coming to Amsterdam.

Evans wouldn't be that naïve, though, would he? After I warned him?

Perhaps not. But there's no way of knowing for sure. I should have made even more of a point of telling him to keep his damn mouth shut. If Garwood found out that Evans is meeting me . . .

Cochran began to walk even faster. And the speed of his thoughts accelerated with his footsteps. It *had* to be Garwood. Garwood had learned from Arlen that Cochran carried the Ardmore Properties money in a vest. That was why the thief had undressed him. That was why the thief hadn't thought of a second suitcase.

Cochran recalled a remark that one of the other Special Agents in the Treasury Department had once made to him: it wasn't the professional criminals you had to be personally afraid of; it was the amateurs, the ones who were inexperienced.

And in this instance it *was* an amateur, a man who couldn't successfully commit the simplest kind of robbery.

He turned the corner into Prins Hendrik Kade and saw the station.

The TEE to Munich was called the Rembrandt. It left Amsterdam at 14:14 and arrived in Munich at 23:14.

Cochran turned away from the notice board for the second time and again fought the temptation to buy two tickets for that afternoon. There was no telephone in the unfinished apartment, but he could call Beatrix; Beatrix would drive over to Heren Gracht, collect Ruth, take her to Reijnier Vinkeles Kade, help her pack, bring her to the station.

It was already twenty minutes to twelve, though, and he still hadn't seen Evans. The Holland-Italy Express had been in for two hours. But then, Evans might not have taken the Holland-Italy Express. He might have come by way of Paris, and the first express from Paris didn't arrive in Amsterdam until twelve thirty. Or he might somehow have got himself to Frankfurt; there was a train from Frankfurt that arrived in Amsterdam at eleven fifty-six. Or he might even have decided not to take a train at all, but to count on the weather's clearing and come by plane.

My own fault, Cochran reproached himself. I was in too much of a hurry. A man like Evans can't be pressured; he needs time to think.

Yet on the whole, it seemed to him, he'd explained the situation well enough. If he were Evans, he'd have done what Cochran told him to do.

No, he'd read Evans accurately. Garwood was the one he'd misread. He should have known, when Garwood insisted on his taking the Rheingold, when Garwood specified the exact day of departure. . . .

Cochran checked his watch. Ten minutes to twelve. He decided to take another look inside the restaurant.

Evans wasn't there.

Cochran came down the steps slowly. His fear for his own

safety had gone. There were too many people around him. In a crowd like that, he had nothing to worry about.

But Evans—Evans was another matter. He didn't *know*, didn't *suspect*.

Putting his hand into his pocket, Cochran fingered the key. He'd already made one attempt to take the suitcase from the locker in order to remove the three thousand pounds that belonged to him, but there had been too many people in the area. He would have had to carry the suitcase to the men's washroom in order to open it in privacy; and by the time he brought it back, someone else might have made use of the locker and no other locker might be available.

He walked the length of the concourse. Every locker was in use. He considered the left-luggage room. Then he remembered Ruth's suggestion: forget about the money; leave it where it was, and simply take off.

But another thought chased that one away. Suppose it was Garwood who showed up to claim the suitcase.

Cochran sighed.

Garwood would have the money, Evans would be sitting in Geneva, and . . . and what? What would Evans do?

Ruth was right. Evans was in no position to go to the police.

O.K., if Garwood showed up to claim the suitcase, let him have it.

Abandoning the idea of retrieving his three thousand pounds, Cochran went toward the center of the concourse. He began to think in terms of encountering Garwood instead of Evans.

He saw no one who resembled either man.

A glance at the station clock told him that it was exactly noon. He looked around again, saw no familiar face, and began another complete circuit of the station. It was unproductive.

At twelve thirty he was on the platform when the train from Paris arrived. Evans was not one of the passengers.

At ten minutes to one he decided to place a call to Geneva. It took him eight minutes to locate a telephone and figure out how to put the call through, and fifteen seconds to learn that Peter Evans had checked out of the Hôtel Richemond the preceding afternoon.

At one thirty Cochran left the station. There was, he thought, nothing else he could do.

Cautiously, O'Rourke followed.

43

Ruth took one look at him and said, "Something went wrong."

Cochran nodded. "He didn't show."

"Oh dear!" She made an effort to smile, but her eyes said: I knew things were too good to last. "What happens now?"

He closed the door behind him and leaned against it for a moment. "I don't know."

She came over to him. He put one arm around her. "I don't know," he said again.

She moved away, but he followed her. "We're stuck here, is that it?" she said.

He took off his coat and hunted for a place to put it. Finally he hung it on a corner of the mantel, but it fell off. He left it on the floor. "He checked out of the hotel in Geneva yesterday. There's been plenty of time for him to get here. I'm afraid he might have been . . . intercepted."

"And that's bad?"

"It could be. . . . On the way to the station, I thought I had things all figured out. I thought I under*stood.* Then at

the station, I thought—well, maybe the *lawyer* would show."
He took the key to the locker from his pocket and glared at
it. "One lousy key, and no one to give it to."

"Perhaps he misunderstood, John. Perhaps he thought you
meant twelve midnight."

Cochran shook his head and put the key back in his pocket.
"I don't think so." He sighed. "I was going to surprise you.
There's a TEE to Munich at a little after two. I was going
to phone Beatrix. I was going to tell her . . . Oh hell, what
difference does it make now? The poor dumb son of a bitch
got waylaid. Or maybe he got scared and went back to England. . . . I suppose I'll have to call the lawyer. He's probably
in London, after all."

"But someone *did* try to steal the money, John."

"I know. And a little while ago I thought I had the answer.
Now . . ." His voice trailed off.

There was a knock at the door.

"That must be Mrs. Joorst," Ruth said. "I'll get it." She
crossed the room and turned the knob. Then, as the door
flew open, she gave a stifled cry.

O'Rourke grabbed her around the waist, put the knife to
her throat and kicked the door shut.

Cochran took a step forward.

"Stop, or I'll cut her," O'Rourke said.

Cochran went rigid. "Hurt her," he said through clenched
teeth, "and I'll kill you."

"Over there, Mr. Smuggler," O'Rourke said. "By the fireplace. That's right. Nice and slow. All the way. That's a good
chap."

Cochran felt the edge of the mantelpiece against his shoulderblades, and stopped. The same man, he thought. The same
man. Then his mind seemed to congeal, along with his body.

"The money," O'Rourke said. "You were hanging about
the storage lockers. That's where it's at now, isn't it? In one
of the storage lockers. Thought you were being clever, didn't

you, Mr. Big American Smuggler? Thought no one would know."

Cochran's eyes were on Ruth. Her face was ashen, and her body was arched backward, but O'Rourke was keeping the blade of the knife against her throat. The slightest movement on her part, and the knife would draw blood. Cochran willed her to remain absolutely still. And willed himself to do the same.

His reasoning ability began to function again. Once more he became aware of the ledge against his back. He realized that the topcoat lay at his feet. He remembered that there were leftover tiles on the mantelpiece. But he ordered himself to do nothing.

No gun, he thought. No gun yesterday, no gun today. Simple weapons. A street criminal, a bully, probably unstable. The type that's truly dangerous. No gun, though. No access to guns. No experience with them. Not a member of any organized gang . . . He's smiling. He's pleased with himself. You smile too. Smile and use words.

"Garwood won't let you get away with this," he said, and was surprised by the quality of his own voice; he sounded calm and friendly. "Garwood isn't what he used to be, but he still has connections. You want to be careful of him."

O'Rourke's smile broadened. "Garwood's dead, I heard. Someone did him in. What do you think of that, Mr. American? Big Mr. Garwood, with all his connections, ain't here anymore."

"But Mr. Evans is. And it's Evans's money. Evans is a very rich man. One of the oldest families in England. He won't like it a bit if he doesn't get his money."

"Rich, is he? Old family, is he? Well now, Mr. American, Mr. Evans is with Mr. Garwood, I heard. The two of them— both taken, they've been. Surprise you?"

"Kind of." Cochran's eyes fastened on Ruth again. He wanted to scream at her: Don't make a move, don't make a sound. But the instructions appeared to be unnecessary; she was handling herself well. "Can't say that I'm particularly sorry, though. Didn't much care for either of them. Not my kind. Not your kind either, I guess."

"No, not my kind either," O'Rourke agreed. Suddenly his smile vanished. His expression became deadly. "The money, Mr. Smuggler, where is it?"

"Just where you think it is. You must have been watching me. You must be very good at watching people. I had no idea you were there. Not the slightest. The money is in a suitcase, a green suitcase. Three hundred and fifty-three thousand pounds."

O'Rourke's face brightened. He moistened his lips with his tongue. "Which locker?"

"I'm not sure exactly. Third or fourth from the right. Third, I believe. Bottom row. The number is on the key, though. You won't have any trouble finding it."

"Naturally," said O'Rourke. "Now give me the key, Mr. American, like a good chap."

"Certainly. But it's in my coat." He made the barest hint of a gesture with his head. "On the floor. I'll have to bend down to pick it up. Is that all right with you?"

There was a flicker of indecision in O'Rourke's eyes. Only a flicker. "Yes. Pick it up. But slowly. Very slowly. Any tricks, and your pretty ladyfriend here gets her throat ventilated. Understand?"

"Perfectly," said Cochran. He went cold with the deepest rage he'd ever experienced. It made his vision blur. He kept the rage out of his voice, however. "You're the boss."

In slow motion he bent his knees and reached out with his left hand. His fingers came into contact with the coat. They closed around it gingerly, and, still in slow motion, he straightened. Carefully he put his hand into the right pocket, frowned, put his hand into the left. "What the hell," he said, puzzled. "Must be in my jacket." He reached into the pocket of his jacket. "Ah, yes." He produced the key and held it out in his outstretched right hand, continuing to hold the topcoat with his left. "What do you want me to do with it?"

"Throw it on the floor," O'Rourke directed. "Your lady-friend will pick it up—won't you, love?"

"Do as he says," Cochran told her quickly. A second wave of rage swept over him. He threw the key. It landed halfway between them.

"Right," said O'Rourke. Then he addressed himself to Ruth. "We'll move together. You pick up the key. I'll take it from you."

As one, they took three steps forward. Ruth's eyes were on Cochran. He nodded reassuringly. She knelt. O'Rourke knelt with her. The knife didn't waver. Cochran noted that he'd never seen a steadier hand. Ruth picked up the key. O'Rourke nudged her to her feet. In unison the two of them stood up.

"Put the key in my hand, love," O'Rourke said.

Ruth's hand moved toward the fingers that were pressed against her abdomen. She touched them with the key. They grasped it.

"Handsome," said O'Rourke.

This, Cochran knew, was the crucial moment. O'Rourke had undoubtedly seen the workmen. He'd probably seen Mrs. Joorst too. It must have been Mrs. Joorst who had told him which apartment Cochran was in. With a knife at Ruth's throat, O'Rourke would know he couldn't get far. He would have to leave the building alone, and with the assurance that neither Cochran nor Ruth could call attention to him. But while he was stabbing one, he was in danger from the other.

Ruth was the one who had to be saved.

"I think you're going to have a bit of trouble getting out of here," Cochran said. "Carpenters, masons all over the place. Slight problem, isn't it? You might need some help."

"Shut up," O'Rourke said. There was uncertainty in his voice, though.

"After all," Cochran went on, "it's not my money. It never was my money. It was Evans's. And Garwood was trying to get it from him. I was just the courier. I have no interest in it. Never did have. But I don't suppose you believe that. You probably think I want to grab it for myself, and I don't suppose there's any way of convincing you I don't, but the truth is, I'd be glad to walk out of here with you, even go down to the station with you. I'd be glad to help you all the way. The trouble is, there's nothing I can say that will make you believe me. So you've kind of a big problem. You might be able to let yourself down from the window, perhaps. It isn't very high. Ten, fifteen feet, I'd say. But that wouldn't be such a good idea. You might break an ankle or something. Or I guess you could lock us in the closet. There's a closet off the bedroom. On the other hand, the very best idea would be for the two of us to go down to the station together and—"

"Shut up. Where's the bedroom?"

"To your left. Past the kitchen." Cochran turned his head. The tiles were out of reach. He uttered a silent oath.

O'Rourke moved sideways. "This way, love," he said to Ruth. "Slowly. Just move with me. That's a good girl. You too," he said to Cochran. "This way. Not too fast. Come one step closer than you are now, and you'll be able to wash your face in the lady's blood."

Cochran followed them, dragging the topcoat, burying his left hand in it.

"Very nice," O'Rourke said. "Just like that. Slow and steady."

"There's no air in the closet," Cochran protested. "We'll suffocate."

"You'll last longer if you keep your mouth shut," O'Rourke said.

They passed the kitchen and went down the narrow hall

that led to the bedroom. O'Rourke saw the closet and the key in the lock. His expression brightened. "You first," he instructed Cochran. "Open the door and get inside."

Cochran opened the door just wide enough to let himself edge through, and as soon as he was inside, he wrapped the coat twice around his left hand and arm.

"Now you," he heard O'Rourke say, and a moment later Ruth slid through the opening.

In one swift movement Cochran shoved her behind him and threw his left shoulder against the door, his left arm crooked in front of him with the coat as a shield.

The sudden weight caught O'Rourke off balance. He staggered backward as the door hit him in the face. Cochran lunged from the closet and threw himself at O'Rourke before he had a chance to recover. The key fell from O'Rourke's hand, but he managed to hang on to the knife and he raised it to strike. Cochran jabbed his knee into O'Rourke's stomach. The knife flew out of O'Rourke's hand as he doubled up. Cochran drove his fist into O'Rourke's face. O'Rourke sank to his knees and reached for the knife. Cochran struck at the outstretched hand with his protected left arm and grasped the wrist with his right, twisting it. O'Rourke gasped with pain. Cochran slammed the outer edge of his right hand against O'Rourke's collarbone. O'Rourke gave a faint sob and fell over on his side.

Cochran picked up the knife, plunged it into O'Rourke's right hand between the thumb and forefinger and made a deep slash. Then, extracting the knife, he stood up, retrieved the key to the locker and placed it in the pocket of O'Rourke's suede coat.

O'Rourke opened his mouth, but no sound came out. His eyes were glazed. His thumb was hanging loosely from the rest of his hand. He clutched his right hand with his left, as if to hold it together.

Cochran dragged him to his feet, gave him a shove that

sent him sprawling against the wall, and raised the knife as if to strike again. O'Rourke threw up his locked hands to protect himself. Blood spurted from his hand and ran down his arm.

"Now get the hell out of here," Cochran said hoarsely.

O'Rourke sidled along the wall toward the front door. Cochran followed him with the upraised knife. O'Rourke had to use both hands to get the door open. Cochran went out to the landing and watched him stumble down the stairs. Then he returned to the apartment and slammed the door. Ruth was standing in the middle of the living room, staring at him.

He swallowed. It was some moments before he could force a smile, and longer before he could speak. "What's the matter?" he said finally. "Haven't you ever seen a Treasury agent at work before?"

She continued to stare at him.

He went to the window and opened it. O'Rourke was lurching down Heren Gracht, in the direction of the station. But as he reached the corner of Burgwal, he collapsed. And just missed being hit by a woman on a bicycle. He tried to get up, but couldn't. He appeared to be losing consciousness. The woman jumped off the bicycle and ran to his aid. She was joined by two pedestrians.

Cochran closed the window. "I guess I severed the radial artery," he said. "If they don't get him to a hospital soon, he'll bleed to death."

Ruth was still standing in the middle of the room, looking at him, wide-eyed. But, he noticed, the color was returning to her face. "See if you can clean up the bloodstains," he said. "I'll ask Mrs. Joorst to drive us to the station. I don't think we ought to hang around here any longer than we absolutely have to, do you?"

"No," she said in a small voice. "But—"

"Now, now," he said soothingly. "There's nothing to worry

about. Everything's going to be all right. I'll explain it all to you on the train. I promise."

And two hours later, as they sped eastward across Holland toward the German border, he kept his promise. It was really very simple, he began; a week ago last Sunday he was sitting in his flat in London, minding his own business, when the telephone rang. . . .

44

There were only thirty passengers on the flight from Amsterdam to Frankfurt.

Klaus Ranken was the first to deplane and the first through passport control. He proceeded down the corridor at a trot, swiftly crossed the concourse and began waving for a taxi even before he reached the taxi rank.

A taxi pulled up. Ranken threw himself into the back seat and, forgetting to give the driver his address, told him to hurry.

"In which direction would you prefer me to go?" the driver asked irritably.

Ranken gave his home address, slammed the door and again told the driver to hurry.

Twenty minutes later he was home.

His two older sons were kicking a ball back and forth across the front yard. They greeted him noisily, demanding to know about his trip.

"Yes, yes," was all he said. "Yes, yes, it was most exciting. I'll tell you about it later."

They followed him into the house. "We want to know about it *now.*"

"Later, I said."

His wife came out of the kitchen. "Klaus! You're back! You should have called! I would have met you!"

He'd only been gone for six hours, but there was more excitement upon his return from this trip than there'd been when he'd come home after three weeks in Scandinavia.

He touched his wife's cheek with his lips, threw his coat on a chair and told her to pour him a glass of wine. "Something special," he added.

"But I want to know—" she began.

"Later, later," he said. "First I must call Ganzhorn."

He picked up the telephone and dialed, and while waiting for the call to go through, he tried to collect his thoughts. There was so much to tell, he didn't know where to begin. He was a hero of sorts, an important witness; an instrument of justice. It was necessary that he not permit himself to be carried away, however. He must comport himself, even over the telephone, with a certain poise, as he'd comported himself in Amsterdam.

Ganzhorn's wife answered.

"Klaus speaking," he said, as unemotionally as he could. "Klaus Ranken. Is Heinz there?"

"Yes."

A moment later Ganzhorn spoke.

"Heinz? Klaus. I'm home. The plane arrived a short while ago." Poise, he reminded himself, and took a deep breath. "It's an astonishing story, Heinz. Really most astonishing. Much larger than anyone had thought. The police met me at Schiphol. They were very considerate, I must say. They took me first to the hospital. Onze Lieve Vrouwe Gasthuis, it was. On Eerste Oosterpark Straat. You know of—"

"What about my car?" Ganzhorn interrupted.

"They haven't found it yet. They appear to think that they will, however. They seem quite certain that it's in Amsterdam. It's simply a matter of time, they think. But the important thing, the really important information, is that I was able to make the identification. It *was* the man who called himself James Howard, Heinz. The man whose real name is Kenneth O'Rourke. He was in very poor condition, but I was able to identify him immediately. *Immediately.* With no hesitation at all. He has a broken nose and a broken collarbone, and an artery in his right hand was severed. He'd been in shock. But when I saw him—"

"Has he confessed to stealing my car?"

"He hasn't confessed to anything. He refuses to speak at all. He simply keeps demanding to see the British Ambassador."

"So—"

"Let me finish. They found in his pocket a key, Heinz. A key to one of the lockers at Amsterdam's Centraal Station. And considering the circumstances, they of course opened the locker, and, Heinz, you'll never guess—you simply can't imagine—what they found."

Ranken's wife brought him the wine, and stood by to listen to the conversation.

"They found a suitcase full of money. More than three hundred and fifty thousand British pounds, Heinz. Two and a quarter million marks!"

This information had the desired effect. "God in heaven!" Ganzhorn cried.

Frau Ranken also said, "God in heaven," adding, "Where did it come from?"

Ranken answered his wife's question as if it had been put to him by Ganzhorn. "He refuses to say where it comes from. He simply says nothing at all."

"He must be one of the terrorists," Ganzhorn ventured.

"The police are considering that possibility. But there is something else that complicates the picture. They have found the body of another Britisher, in one of the canals. They've identified him as a lawyer from London. They think there may be some connection. A quarrel of some sort. The lawyer had been beaten, and O'Rourke had been stabbed in the hand. It's really quite multifaceted, you see. Two Englishmen, a stolen car, all that money. It may, the police think, have been simply a falling out among thieves."

"But the murder, the woman from Karlsruhe—there's no connection, then?"

"Well," said Ranken, "that's problematical. There may be a connection, there may not. You see, among the possessions of this man O'Rourke they found, also in the pocket of his coat, a pair of earrings. Women's earrings. An odd thing for a man to be carrying, of course. They are sending the earrings to Karlsruhe, on the chance that Erika Rebholz's mother may be able to identify them. If she can, well—"

"God in heaven," Ganzhorn said—this time with awe in his voice. "It—it's—" he groped for a word, but was unable to come up with one.

"The work of a twisted mind," Ranken concluded for him, and sipped some of the wine. Composure, he told himself. Dignity. "I sensed *that* as soon as I entered the hospital room. Definitely a twisted mind. For when he saw me, I'm certain he recognized me, just as I recognized him. But instead of denying that he knew me, he simply said, 'You're not the British Ambassador—you're a bloody Kraut.' And then he turned his head away and refused to say anything more. That in itself indicates derangement, don't you think? Not only was it rude, but it was an admission that we'd met before."

"Yes," Ganzhorn agreed. "Undoubtedly a sign of derangement. Nevertheless I hope that he'll be brought to trial."

"The police assured me that they intend to conduct a thorugh investigation. I believe he'll be tried for something. Perhaps the money. Perhaps the earrings. Perhaps the car. Perhaps, even, all three. I'm quite certain of it, Heinz: the man will not go free."

Unexpectedly, Ganzhorn laughed. "I *do* like you, Klaus. I always have. But I must say, you *are* attracted to the most peculiar people. You really are."

"I was merely being friendly," Ranken said stiffly, and with that he put down the telephone, shrugged and finished the wine. The wine, he thought, was actually quite good.

Hand in hand, Cochran and Ruth walked slowly across Marienplatz, looking at the tower of the city hall. It was one minute past eleven in the morning, and the Glockenspiel figures were still doing the Schäffler Dance as the clock chimed. Ruth was enchanted. Giving Cochran's hand a squeeze, she said, delightedly, "Fantasy, darling. Utter fantasy. Straight from the world of make-believe. Don't you love it?"

Cochran grinned. He did love it, but what he loved most of all was Ruth's happiness. In the past two days, she seemed to have shed ten years. Everything was novel and exciting to her. For the first time in longer than she cared to remember, she admitted, she felt as if she didn't have a care in the world. And that was what he liked best about Munich: Ruth's laughter, her shining eyes.

He himself didn't feel quite so carefree. His thoughts wouldn't stay put. They kept darting back to the past, ahead to the future. Had the police found the suitcase with the money? Had the young hood in the suede coat been questioned about it? Had he implicated an American named John Cochran? If he had, did the police believe him?

Unanswered questions, all of them. And Cochran devoutly hoped that he would never have to learn the answers. But there was no way of guessing what the future held.

He recalled the flat on Basil Street, Arlen, the long, empty years in London. By comparison, his existence in Munich would be idyllic.

But the money that he and Ruth had between them would run out. Even if the police didn't pursue him—and he was inclined to think that they might not—there would be other problems, practical problems.

He pictured himself returning to the United States and beginning a new life there as John Cochran. He even pictured himself being married to Ruth, having a regular job, doing what most other people did.

It was conceivable. Anything was conceivable. But he didn't know. All he could do was take each day as it came.

Yet, he reminded himself, his position wasn't all that different from anyone else's. No one knew what kind of hand the future was going to deal. Security was an illusion, a state of mind.

And he had to admit that his state of mind at the moment was better than it had been for years. Part three of his life, he felt, was going to be a distinct improvement over parts one and two.

The clock stopped chiming. The figures ended their dance.

Ruth applauded. Cochran put his arm around her. They walked slowly toward Dienerstrasse.

Ruth paused once to look back, but Cochran urged her on.

"Let's keep going," he said. "There's so much we haven't seen yet."

She nodded, and quickened her pace. "You're right," she agreed. "There really is."